Instructor's Resource Guide for

# PUBLIC SPEAKING

# Instructor's Resource Guide for

# PUBLIC SPEAKING

Michael Osborn and Suzanne Osborn

**Suzanne McCorkle**
*Boise State University*

**HOUGHTON MIFFLIN COMPANY**     **BOSTON**

Dallas     Geneva, Illinois     Princeton, New Jersey     Palo Alto

*Acknowledgment*

Selections from *Winning Orations of the Interstate Oratorical Society*, 1983, reprinted by permission of the Interstate Oratorical Society.

Printed in the U.S.A.

ISBN: 0–395–42726–6

BCDEFGHIJ-B-9543210/898

# CONTENTS

Introduction . . . . . . . . . . . . . . . . . . . . . . . . . . . . xi

## PART I: PLANNING THE DAY-TO-DAY SCHEDULE    1

Sample Syllabi . . . . . . . . . . . . . . . . . . . . . . . . . . 3

Finding Exercises and Supporting Materials . . . . . . . . . . . 6

## PART II: SPEECH ASSIGNMENTS    7

Making Speech Assignments . . . . . . . . . . . . . . . . . . . 9
    Introductory Speech . . . . . . . . . . . . . . . . . 9
    Goal Speech . . . . . . . . . . . . . . . . . . . . . . 9
    Informative Speech with Narrative . . . . . . . . . . . . 9
    Informative Speech . . . . . . . . . . . . . . . . . . . 10
    Informative Speech with Visual Aid . . . . . . . . . . . 10
    Speech of Demonstration . . . . . . . . . . . . . . . 10
    Persuasive Speech . . . . . . . . . . . . . . . . . . . 11
    Short Persuasive Message . . . . . . . . . . . . . . . 11
    Revised Speech . . . . . . . . . . . . . . . . . . . . 12

Forms for Evaluating Speeches . . . . . . . . . . . . . . . . . 13
    Introductory Speech Evaluation Form . . . . . . . . . . 13
    Goal Speech Evaluation Form . . . . . . . . . . . . . 14
    Informative Speech with Narrative Evaluation Form . . . . . . . 15
    Informative Speech Evaluation Form . . . . . . . . . . . 16
    Informative Speech with Visual Aid Evaluation Form . . . . . . . 17
    Speech of Demonstration Evaluation Form . . . . . . . . . 18
    Persuasive Speech Evaluation Form . . . . . . . . . . . 19
    Short Persuasive Message Evaluation Form . . . . . . . . . 20
    Toast Evaluation Form . . . . . . . . . . . . . . . . . 21
    Overall Speech Evaluation Form . . . . . . . . . . . . . 22

**PART III: CHAPTER-BY-CHAPTER GUIDE                    25**

1 / Public Speaking as Communication . . . . . . . . . . . . 27
Chapter Objectives, 27 / Discussion, 28 / Application, 29 / Additional Exercises, 31 /
Additional Resources, 33 / Special Feature: Crossword Puzzle, 33

2 / Your First Speech . . . . . . . . . . . . . . . . . . 37
Chapter Objectives, 37 / Discussion, 38 / Application, 39 / Additional Exercises, 41 /
Preparation Outline Worksheet, 42 / Additional Resources, 43

3 / Critical Listening and Speech Evaluation . . . . . . . . . . 45
Chapter Objectives, 45 / Discussion, 46 / Application, 47 / Additional Exercises, 48 /
Additional Resources, 50 / Special Feature: Crossword Puzzle, 51

4 / Selecting and Researching Your Topic . . . . . . . . . . . 55
Chapter Objectives, 55 / Discussion, 56 / Application, 57 / Additional Exercises, 59 /
Additional Resources, 63

5 / Audience Analysis and Adaptation . . . . . . . . . . . . 65
Chapter Objectives, 65 / Discussion, 66 / Application, 68 / Additional Exercises, 71 /
Attitude Survey, 74 / Audience Analysis Worksheet, 76 / Additional Resources, 80

6 / Audience Analysis and Adaptation . . . . . . . . . . . . 81
Chapter Objectives, 81 / Discussion, 82 / Application, 82 / Additional Exercises, 85 /
Additional Resources, 87

7 / Outlining Your Speech . . . . . . . . . . . . . . . . 89
Chapter Objectives, 89 / Discussion, 90 / Application, 90 / Additional Exercises, 92 /
Additional Resources, 93 / Outline Scramble, 94 / Unscrambled Outline, 96

8 / Visual Aids . . . . . . . . . . . . . . . . . . . . 99
Chapter Objectives, 99 / Discussion, 100 / Application, 101 / Additional Exercises,
102 / Additional Resources, 105

9 / The Speaker's Language . . . . . . . . . . . . . . . . 107
Chapter Objectives, 107 / Discussion, 108 / Application, 109 / Additional Exercises,
111 / Additional Resources, 113

10 / Presenting Your Speech . . . . . . . . . . . . . . . . 115
Chapter Objectives, 115 / Discussion, 116 / Application, 117 / Voice and Appearance
Checklist, 119 / Additional Exercises, 120 / Additional Resources, 123

11 / The Nature and Kinds of Informative Speaking . . . . . . . 125
Chapter Objectives, 125 / Discussion, 125 / Application, 127 / Additional Exercises,
128 / Additional Resources, 129

12 / The Use of Supporting Materials . . . . . . . . . . . . 131
Chapter Objectives, 131 / Discussion, 132 / Application, 133 / Additional Exercises,
135 / Additional Resources, 136

13 / The Nature and Kinds of Persuasive Speaking . . . . . . . 139
Chapter Objectives, 139 / Discussion, 140 / Application, 141 / Additional Exercises,
143 / Additional Resources, 144

14 / Evidence, Proof, and Argument . . . . . . . . . . . . . 145
Chapter Objectives, 145 / Discussion, 146 / Application, 148 / Additional Exercises,
149 / Additional Resources, 150 / Special Feature: Crossword Puzzle, 151

15 / Ceremonial Speaking . . . . . . . . . . . . . . . . . . 155
Chapter Objectives, 155 / Discussion, 155 / Application, 157 / Additional Exercises,
158 / Additional Resources, 160

Appendix A / Group Communication . . . . . . . . . . . . 161
Observations, 161 / Additional Resources, 161

**PART IV: TEST QUESTIONS**                                  **163**
Some Notes on Testing . . . . . . . . . . . . . . . . . 165

1 / Public Speaking as Communication . . . . . . . . . . 166
True-False Questions . . . . . . . . . . . . . . . . . . 166
Multiple-Choice Questions . . . . . . . . . . . . . . . 167
Short-Answer Questions . . . . . . . . . . . . . . . . 172
Essay Questions . . . . . . . . . . . . . . . . . . . . 173

2 / Your First Speech . . . . . . . . . . . . . . . . . . 174
True-False Questions . . . . . . . . . . . . . . . . . . 174
Multiple-Choice Questions . . . . . . . . . . . . . . . 175
Short-Answer Questions . . . . . . . . . . . . . . . . 179
Essay Questions . . . . . . . . . . . . . . . . . . . . 180

3 / Critical Listening and Speech Evaluation . . . . . . . 181
True-False Questions . . . . . . . . . . . . . . . . . . 181
Multiple-Choice Questions . . . . . . . . . . . . . . . 182
Short-Answer Questions . . . . . . . . . . . . . . . . 187
Essay Questions . . . . . . . . . . . . . . . . . . . . 188

4 / Selecting and Researching Your Topic . . . . . . . . . 189
True-False Questions . . . . . . . . . . . . . . . . . . 189
Multiple-Choice Questions . . . . . . . . . . . . . . . 191
Short-Answer Questions . . . . . . . . . . . . . . . . 196
Essay Questions . . . . . . . . . . . . . . . . . . . . 197

5 / Audience Analysis and Adaptation . . . . . . . . . . 198
True-False Questions . . . . . . . . . . . . . . . . . . 198
Multiple-Choice Questions . . . . . . . . . . . . . . . 200
Short-Answer Questions . . . . . . . . . . . . . . . . 205
Essay Questions . . . . . . . . . . . . . . . . . . . . 206

6 / Structuring Your Speech . . . . . . . . . . . . . . . 207
True-False Questions . . . . . . . . . . . . . . . . . . 207
Multiple-Choice Questions . . . . . . . . . . . . . . . 209
Short-Answer Questions . . . . . . . . . . . . . . . . 213
Essay Questions . . . . . . . . . . . . . . . . . . . . 214

7 / Outlining Your Speech . . . . . . . . . . . . . . . . 215
True-False Questions . . . . . . . . . . . . . . . . . . 215
Multiple-Choice Questions . . . . . . . . . . . . . . . 216
Short-Answer Questions . . . . . . . . . . . . . . . . 220
Essay Questions . . . . . . . . . . . . . . . . . . . . 221

8 / Visual Aids . . . . . . . . . . . . . . . . . . . . . . 222
True-False Questions . . . . . . . . . . . . . . . . . . 222
Multiple-Choice Questions . . . . . . . . . . . . . . . 223
Short-Answer Questions . . . . . . . . . . . . . . . . 227
Essay Questions . . . . . . . . . . . . . . . . . . . . 228

9 / The Speaker's Language . . . . . . . . . . . . . . . .229
    True-False Questions . . . . . . . . . . . . . . . . 229
    Multiple-Choice Questions . . . . . . . . . . . . . 230
    Short-Answer Questions . . . . . . . . . . . . . . 235
    Essay Questions . . . . . . . . . . . . . . . . . . 236

10 / Presenting Your Speech . . . . . . . . . . . . . . .237
    True-False Questions . . . . . . . . . . . . . . . . 237
    Multiple-Choice Questions . . . . . . . . . . . . . 239
    Short-Answer Questions . . . . . . . . . . . . . . 244
    Essay Questions . . . . . . . . . . . . . . . . . . 245

11 / The Nature and Kinds of Informative Speaking . . . . . .246
    True-False Questions . . . . . . . . . . . . . . . . 246
    Multiple-Choice Questions . . . . . . . . . . . . . 247
    Short-Answer Questions . . . . . . . . . . . . . . 251
    Essay Questions . . . . . . . . . . . . . . . . . . 252

12 / The Use of Supporting Materials . . . . . . . . . . .253
    True-False Questions . . . . . . . . . . . . . . . . 253
    Multiple-Choice Questions . . . . . . . . . . . . . 254
    Short-Answer Questions . . . . . . . . . . . . . . 259
    Essay Questions . . . . . . . . . . . . . . . . . . 260

13 / The Nature and Kinds of Persuasive Speaking . . . . . . 261
    True-False Questions . . . . . . . . . . . . . . . . 261
    Multiple-Choice Questions . . . . . . . . . . . . . 263
    Short-Answer Questions . . . . . . . . . . . . . . 267
    Essay Questions . . . . . . . . . . . . . . . . . . 268

14 / Evidence, Proof, and Argument . . . . . . . . . . . .269
    True-False Questions . . . . . . . . . . . . . . . . 269
    Multiple-Choice Questions . . . . . . . . . . . . . 270
    Short-Answer Questions . . . . . . . . . . . . . . 276
    Essay Questions . . . . . . . . . . . . . . . . . . 277

15 / Ceremonial Speaking . . . . . . . . . . . . . . . . .278
    True-False Questions . . . . . . . . . . . . . . . . 278
    Multiple-Choice Questions . . . . . . . . . . . . . 280
    Short-Answer Questions . . . . . . . . . . . . . . 285
    Essay Questions . . . . . . . . . . . . . . . . . . 286

Appendix A / Group Communication . . . . . . . . . . . .287
    True-False Questions . . . . . . . . . . . . . . . . 287
    Multiple-Choice Questions . . . . . . . . . . . . . 288
    Short-Answer Questions . . . . . . . . . . . . . . 291
    Essay Questions . . . . . . . . . . . . . . . . . . 292

**PART V: ANSWER KEYS FOR TEST QUESTIONS**     **293**

1 / Public Speaking as Communication . . . . . . . . . . .295

2 / Your First Speech . . . . . . . . . . . . . . . . . .295

3 / Critical Listening and Speech Evaluation . . . . . . .296

4 / Selecting and Researching Your Topic . . . . . . . . .296

5 / Audience Analysis and Adaptation . . . . . . . . . . 297

6 / Structuring Your Speech . . . . . . . . . . . . 297

7 / Outlining Your Speech . . . . . . . . . . . . 298

8 / Visual Aids . . . . . . . . . . . . . . . . 299

9 / The Speaker's Language . . . . . . . . . . . . 299

10 / Presenting Your Speech . . . . . . . . . . . . 300

11 / The Nature and Kinds of Informative Speaking . . . . . . 300

12 / The Use of Supporting Materials . . . . . . . . . 301

13 / The Nature and Kinds of Persuasive Speaking . . . . . . 301

14 / Evidence, Proof, and Argument . . . . . . . . . 302

15 / Ceremonial Speaking . . . . . . . . . . . . 302

Appendix A / Group Communication . . . . . . . . . 303

## PART VI: TRANSPARENCY PACKAGE — 305

List of Transparencies . . . . . . . . . . . . . . 307

## APPENDIXES — 309

A / Sample Introductions . . . . . . . . . . . . 311

B / Sample Conclusions . . . . . . . . . . . . . 314

C / Two Formal Outlines . . . . . . . . . . . . . 316
"Sheathing the Silent Knife" by Trevor S. Giles . . . . . . . . 316
"As Time Goes By" by Brian Welch . . . . . . . . . . 318

D / Analysis of Student Speeches in Appendix B of
PUBLIC SPEAKING . . . . . . . . . . . . . 321
"The Right Fuel" by Thressia Taylor . . . . . . . . . 321
"Are the Skies That Friendly?" by Juli Pardell . . . . . . . . 321
"The Gift of Life" by Paul B. Fowler . . . . . . . . . 321
"Sheathing the Silent Knife" by Trevor S. Giles . . . . . . . . 321
"As Time Goes By" by Brian Welch . . . . . . . . . 322

E / Places to Find Additional Speech Texts . . . . . . . . 323

# INTRODUCTION

The *Instructor's Resource Guide* for PUBLIC SPEAKING includes information that both new and experienced teachers should find useful in their classrooms. Parts I and II contain materials for organizing the public speaking curriculum—sample syllabi, grading criteria for evaluating speeches, and speech evaluation forms that can be easily torn out and duplicated for use by students. Part III is a chapter-by-chapter guide to PUBLIC SPEAKING by Michael and Suzanne Osborn. For each chapter, it offers chapter objectives, suggestions for using and responding to the Discussion and Application questions, and additional exercises and readings. Part IV contains a generous number of true-false, multiple-choice, short-answer, and essay questions for each chapter of the text; answers to the objective test questions are provided (in an easy-to-duplicate format) in Part V. Part VI contains a list of nineteen acetate transparencies for use with an overhead projector; these transparencies are available to adopters of PUBLIC SPEAKING. The *Instructor's Resource Guide* ends with appendixes containing sample introductions and conclusions, two formal outlines and five brief analyses of the student speeches in Appendix B of PUBLIC SPEAKING, and suggested places to find additional speech texts for classroom use.

*Part I*

---

# PLANNING THE DAY-TO-DAY SCHEDULE

# SAMPLE SYLLABI

Course title _____

Instructor's name _____

Office location _____

Phone _____ Office hours _____

## POLICIES

1. No make-up speeches or tests will be allowed unless approved in advance. (Call when you are ill.)

2. Both listening and speech evaluation are important. Therefore, excessive absences will adversely affect your grade.

3. To pass the course, all assignments must be completed.

4. A formal outline (when assigned) is due at the beginning of the class in which you are scheduled to speak.

5. Plagiarism of any speech will result in a failing grade.

6. All speeches must be presented extemporaneously (not written out or memorized), unless otherwise assigned.

7. Do not bring any potentially dangerous visual aid materials (such as explosives or weapons) to class, unless you have checked with the instructor beforehand.

8. Grading will be on a straight scale as follows:

   A = 90–100%

   B = 80–89%

   C = 70–79%

   D = 60–69%

   F = 0–59%

9. Points will be distributed as follows (use speech types assigned):

   | | |
   |---|---|
   | Introductory speech (3–5 minutes) | 50 |
   | Goal speech (3–5 minutes) | 50 |
   | Informative speech with narrative (3–5 minutes) | 100 |
   | Informative speech (3–5 minutes) | 100 |
   | Informative speech with visual aid (3–5 minutes) | 100 |
   | Speech of demonstration (4–6 minutes) | 100 |

Persuasive speech (5–7 minutes)                    150
Short persuasive message (1–1½ minutes)             50
Toast (1–3 minutes)                                 50

## 10-Week Course*—4 Days per Week

| Day | Assignment |
| --- | --- |
| 1 | Orientation/Syllabus |
| 2 | Chapter 1 |
| 3 | Chapter 2 |
| 4 | Chapter 3 |
| 5 | Chapter 4 |
| 6 | Chapter 5 |
| 7–10 | Introductory Speeches (6 per day, plus critiques/discussion) |
| 11–12 | Chapters 6 and 7 |
| 13–14 | Chapters 8, 9, and 10 |
| 15–16 | Chapters 11 and 12 |
| 17 | Catch-up and Review |
| 18 | Midterm Exam |
| 19–23 | Informative Speeches (5 per day, plus critiques/discussion) |
| 24–26 | Chapters 13 and 14 |
| 27–32 | Persuasive Speeches (4-5 per day, plus critiques/discussion) |
| 33 | Chapter 15 |
| 34–37 | Ceremonial Speeches (6 per day, plus critiques/discussion) |
| 38–40 | Optional Assignments |

* Use time alloted for final exam to have final-round speeches (3–4 minutes, type and topic of speaker'schoice)

## 14-Week Course*—3 Days per Week

| Day | Assignment |
| --- | --- |
| 1 | Orientation/Syllabus |
| 2 | Chapter 1 |
| 3 | Chapter 2 |
| 4 | Chapter 3 |
| 5 | Chapter 4 |
| 6 | Chapter 5 |
| 7–9 | Introductory Speeches (3–5 minutes) |
| 10 | Quiz (Chapters 1–5); Begin Chapters 6 and 7 |
| 11–12 | Chapters 6 and 7 |
| 13–14 | Chapters 8, 9, and 10 |
| 15–16 | Chapters 11 and 12 |
| 17 | Quiz (Chapters 6–12) |
| 18–21 | Informative Speeches (3–5 minutes) |
| 22 | Review Informative Speeches from Days 18–21 |
| 23–27 | Informative Speeches (3–5 minutes) |
| 28–30 | Chapters 13 and 14 |
| 31–36 | Persuasive Speeches (5–7 minutes) |
| 37–38 | Chapter 15 |
| 39–41 | Ceremonial Speeches (3–5 minutes) |
| 42 | Quiz (Chapters 13–15) |

* Use time alloted for final exam to have final-round speeches (3–4 minutes, type and topic of speaker's choice)

## SAMPLE SYLLABI AS ASSIGNMENT GUIDES

The sample syllabi above are day-to-day assignment guides that could be modified for distribution to students. The instructor should convert the day numbers to dates (allowing for holidays and days missed while at conventions) and make adjustments to suit personal preferences.

Many instructors will opt to prepare two day-to-day assignment guides: one for students and one for the instructor. The instructor's guide would also include a schedule of what assignments to make, concepts to cover, and exercises to use in class.

# FINDING EXERCISES AND SUPPORTING MATERIALS

Colleagues who teach the same or similar courses are the best sources for discovering (and discussing) new strategies for presenting materials. Professional meetings and swap sessions can also be wellsprings of new ideas. Unfortunately, not all of us have colleagues with whom to share information when we need it.

Another good source of ideas is professional literature. Several journals regularly discuss instructional methods. For example, *Communication Education* runs a section called Instructional Practices. Other journals, such as *Communication Quarterly*, occasionally focus on instructional practices. Two other publications that might prove helpful are: Douglas Bock and E. Hope Bock, *Evaluating Classroom Speaking* (Annandale, VA.: Speech Communication Association, 1981); and J. William Pfeiffer and John E. Jones, *A Handbook of Structured Experiences for Human Relations Training* (University Associates, La Jolla, CA, published annually). In addition, the Speech Communication Association (5105 Backlick Road, Building E, Annandale, Virginia 22003; 703-750-0533) and regional associations may provide brochures listing a variety of useful materials and publications.

*Part II*

# ASSIGNMENTS

# MAKING SPEECH ASSIGNMENTS

Each speech assignment carries a time limit, brief description, and list of grading criteria. The grading criteria are incremental; new skills are required with each speech. Delivery is not included as a grading criterion on the evaluation forms until several speeches have been delivered. The incremental approach is based on the premise that students can focus on one skill at a time—organization, introduction, conclusion, evidence, eye contact, gestures, and so forth. However, you should use the evaluation form to comment on all aspects of a speech. Under the additional comments section of each form, include some positive and some negative comments. Following the forms for individual speech assignments is an Overall Speech Evaluation Form. The text authors encourage you to duplicate this, and the other forms, for use in class.

## INTRODUCTORY SPEECH

**Time:** 3–5 minutes

**Assignment:** Using the guide in Chapter 2, prepare an introductory speech that focuses on the area that best identifies you as the person you are introducing.

**Grading criteria:** Focus on one area for development; clear purpose and thematic statement; appropriate organizational design; speech introduction gains attention; speaker credibility is enhanced; conclusion creates closure, bringing speech to a satisfying end.

## GOAL SPEECH

**Time:** 3–5 minutes

**Assignment:** Develop a speech that focuses on a personal goal.

**Grading criteria:** Topic is appropriately narrowed, introduction gains attention, clear purpose and thematic statement, material sustains audience interest, appropriate organizational design, conclusion creates closure.

## INFORMATIVE SPEECH WITH NARRATIVE

**Time:** 3–5 minutes

**Assignment:** Present an informative speech about an experience youremember vividly. Use suggestions from Chapter 4 to select your topic. During your description of the experience, use a narrative toexplain and create identification with the audience. In your introduction, give the audience reasons to be interested in your topic ("Why should we care?").

**Grading criteria:** Topic is appropriately narrowed and well suited foraudience and occasion, introduction gains attention, clear purpose and thematic statement, material sustains audience interest, appropriateorganizational design, narrative is used and properly developed, conclusion creates closure.

## INFORMATIVE SPEECH

**Time:** 3–5 minutes

**Assignment:** Inform the audience about a topic of your choice. Yourspeech should demonstrate clear organization and use documented supporting materials.

**Grading criteria:** Topic is well suited for audience and occasion, topicis adapted to audience, introduction is dynamic and fulfills functions, clear purpose and thematic statement, appropriate and clear organizational design, transitions are clear, sources are wellselected, and conclusion is effective.

## INFORMATIVE SPEECH WITH VISUAL AID

**Time:** 3–5 minutes

**Assignment:** Select a topic that can be enhanced by the use of avisual aid. Your speech should demonstrate clear organization, andthe visual aid must enhance the message.

**Grading criteria:** Topic is well suited for audience and occasion, topicis adapted to audience, dynamic introduction fulfills its functions, clear purpose and thematic statement, appropriate and clear organizational design, clear transitions, sources are well selected,visual aid is well constructed and enhances message, conclusion is effective.

## SPEECH OF DEMONSTRATION

**Time:** 4–6 minutes

**Assignment:** Inform the audience about a topic that involves the demonstration of a skill or process. You must make a demonstration during the speech.

**Grading criteria:** Topic is well suited for audience and occasion, topic is adapted to audience, dynamic introduction fulfills its functions, clear purpose and thematic statement, appropriate and well-planned demonstration, good transitions, well-chosen sources, appropriate use of language, effective conclusion.

## PERSUASIVE SPEECH

**Time:** 5–7 minutes

**Assignment:** Deliver a persuasive speech on a topic that is appropriate for the audience. Use effective language, a dynamic delivery, and a variety of supporting materials to achieve your specific purpose.

**Grading criteria:** Topic and purpose are appropriate for audience and occasion, topic is adapted to audience, dynamic introduction fulfills its functions, clear purpose and thematic statement, appropriate and clear organizational design, clear transitions, well-chosen sources, effective language enhances persuasive message, various supporting materials are used, eye contact and gestures enhance message, conclusion summarizes arguments.

## SHORT PERSUASIVE MESSAGE

**Time:** 1–1$\frac{1}{2}$ minutes

**Assignment:** Create a persuasive public service message to be broadcast on radio or television.

**Grading criteria:** Appropriate topic and purpose for local community; dynamic introduction fulfills its functions; clear purpose and thematic statement; appropriate and clear design; clear transitions; effective language enhances persuasive message; various supporting materials are used; appropriate vocal variety, rate, and pitch; conclusion summarizes arguments and advocates action.

## TOAST

**Time:** 1–3 minutes

**Assignment:** Prepare a toast for a meritorious person, alive or dead. The toast should fulfill the characteristics of toasts described in Chapter 15.

**Grading criteria:** Introduction gains attention, person being toasted is clearly named, creation of identification between person being toasted and audience, language is used to magnify, delivery is appropriately dynamic, memorized presentation is used effectively, conclusion creates closure.

## REVISED SPEECH

**Time:** 4–6 minutes

**Assignment:** Select any of your speeches with which you were notcompletely satisfied (because of poor introduction, insufficient organization, lack of source documentation, or poor conclusion, forexample). Revise the speech to correct any problems or deficiencies. Further enhance the speech, using what you have learned since itsoriginal delivery. Turn in the evaluation form from your first attempt.

**Grading criteria:** Significant improvement over the original versionof the speech, plus all the relevant content and delivery criteria for the type of speech selected.

# FORMS FOR EVALUATING SPEECHES

## INTRODUCTORY SPEECH EVALUATION FORM

**Speaker's name** _____     **Topic** _____

Introduction gains attention:                     ____ (10)

Specific purpose and thematic statement are clear:   ____ (10)

Organizational design is appropriate:             ____ (5)

Speaker credibility is enhanced:                  ____ (5)

Conclusion creates closure:                       ____ (10)

General impression:                               ____ (10)

                                                  ____ (50 total points)

Time _____ (3–5 minutes)

Additional comments:

## GOAL SPEECH EVALUATION FORM

**Speaker's name** _____          **Topic** _____

Topic is narrowed:                                        ____ (10)

Introduction gains attention:                             ____ (5)

Specific purpose and thematic statement are clear:        ____ (5)

Material sustains audience interest:                      ____ (5)

Organizational design is appropriate:                    ____ (10)

Conclusion creates closure:                              ____ (5)

General impression:                                      ____ (10)

                                                         ____ (50 total points)

Time _____ (3–5 minutes)

Additional comments:

## INFORMATIVE SPEECH WITH NARRATIVE EVALUATION FORM

**Speaker's name** _____     **Topic** _____

Topic is narrowed and well suited for audience/occasion:     ____ (10)

Introduction gains attention:     ____ (10)

Specific purpose and thematic statement are clear:     ____ (10)

Material sustains audience interest:     ____ (10)

Organizational design is appropriate:     ____ (10)

Narrative is used:     ____ (20)

Conclusion creates closure:     ____ (10)

General impression:     ____ (20)

____ (100 total points)

Time ____ (3–5 minutes)

Additional comments:

## INFORMATIVE SPEECH EVALUATION FORM

**Speaker's name**_____     **Topic**_____

Topic is well suited for audience/occasion:     ____ (10)

Topic is adapted to audience:     ____ (10)

Introduction is dynamic and fulfills functions:     ____ (10)

Specific purpose and thematic statement are clear:     ____ (10)

Organizational design is appropriate and clear:     ____ (10)

Speaker credibility is enhanced:     ____ (10)

Transitions are clear:     ____ (10)

Sources are well chosen and documented:     ____ (10)

Conclusion is effective:     ____ (10)

General impression:     ____ (10)

____ (100 total points)

Time ____ (3–5 minutes)

Additional comments:

## INFORMATIVE SPEECH WITH VISUAL AID EVALUATION FORM

**Speaker's name**_____     **Topic** _____

| | |
|---|---|
| Topic is well suited for audience/occasion: | ____ (10) |
| Topic is adapted to audience: | ____ (5) |
| Introduction is dynamic and fulfills functions: | ____ (10) |
| Specific purpose and thematic statement are clear: | ____ (10) |
| Organizational design is appropriate and clear: | ____ (15) |
| Speaker credibility is enhanced: | ____ (5) |
| Transitions are clear: | ____ (5) |
| Sources are well chosen and documented: | ____ (10) |
| Visual aid enhances message and is well constructed: | ____ (15) |
| Conclusion is effective: | ____ (5) |
| General impression: | ____ (10) |
| | ____ (100 total points) |

Time ____ (3–5 minutes)

Additional comments:

## SPEECH OF DEMONSTRATION EVALUATION FORM

**Speaker's name**_____     **Topic**_____

Topic is well suited for audience/occasion:            ____ (5)

Topic is adapted to audience:                          ____ (5)

Introduction is dynamic and fulfills functions:       ____ (10)

Specific purpose and thematic statement are clear:    ____ (10)

Demonstration is appropriate and well organized:      ____ (20)

Speaker credibility is enhanced:                      ____ (5)

Transitions are clear:                                ____ (5)

Sources are well chosen and documented:               ____ (10)

Language is used appropriately:                       ____ (10)

Conclusion is effective:                              ____ (10)

General impression:                                   ____ (10)

                                                      ____ (100 total points)

Time ____ (4–6 minutes)

Additional comments:

# PERSUASIVE SPEECH EVALUATION FORM

**Speaker's name**_____     **Topic**_____

Topic and purpose are well suited for audience/occasion: ____ (10)

Topic is adapted to audience: ____ (5)

Introduction is dynamic and fulfills functions: ____ (10)

Specific purpose and thematic statement are clear: ____ (10)

Organizational design is appropriate and clear: ____ (15)

Speaker credibility is enhanced: ____ (5)

Transitions are clear: ____ (5)

Sources are well chosen and documented: ____ (10)

Language enhances persuasive message: ____ (20)

Variety of supporting materials is used: ____ (20)

Eye contact enhances message: ____ (10)

Gesture and body movement enhance message: ____ (10)

Conclusion summarizes arguments: ____ (10)

General impression: ____ (10)

____ (150 total points)

Time ____ (5–7 minutes)

Additional comments:

## SHORT PERSUASIVE MESSAGE EVALUATION FORM

**Speaker's name**_____     **Topic**_____

Topic and purpose are well suited for audience/occasion:     ____ (5)

Introduction is dynamic and fulfills functions:     ____ (5)

Specific purpose and thematic statement are clear:     ____ (5)

Organizational design is appropriate and clear:     ____ (10)

Transitions are clear:     ____ (5)

Vocal variety, pitch, and rate enhance message:     ____ (5)

Conclusion summarizes arguments and advocates action:     ____ (5)

Stays within time constraints:     ____ (5)

General impression:     ____ (5)

____ (50 total points)

Time ____ (1–1$\frac{1}{2}$ minutes)

Additional comments:

## TOAST EVALUATION FORM

**Speaker's name** _____     **Occasion** _____

Introduction gains attention:                              ____ (5)

Person being toasted is clearly named:                     ____ (5)

Identification is created between person
   being toasted and audience:                         ____ (10)

Language is used to magnify:                               ____ (5)

Delivery is appropriately dynamic:                         ____ (15)

Memorized presentation is used effectively:               ____ (5)

Conclusion creates closure:                                ____ (5)

                                                   ____ (50 total points)

Time ____ (1–3 minutes)

Additional comments:

# OVERALL SPEECH EVALUATION FORM

**Comments**

**Commitment**

_____ Did the speaker seem committed to the topic?

_____ Had the speaker done enough research?

**Topic**

_____ Was the topic worthwhile?

_____ Did the topic fit the assignment and time limit?

**Purpose**

_____ Was the purpose of the speech clear?

**Audience Involvement**

_____ Was the topic adapted to the audience?

_____ Were you able to identify with the speaker and the topic?

**Substance**

_____ Was the speech meaningful to you?

_____ Was the topic handled imaginatively?

_____ Were the main points supported by evidence?

_____ Were the examples clear and interesting?

_____ Was the reasoning clear and correct?

**Structure**

_____ Did the introduction arouse your interest?

_____ Was the speech easy to follow?

_____ Was important information emphasized?

_____ Were transitions used to tie the speech together?

_____ Did the conclusion help you remember the message?

**Language**

_____ Was the language clear, simple, and direct?

_____ Were grammar and pronounciations correct?

_____ Was the language concrete and colorful?

**Presentation**

_____ Was the speaker enthusiastic?

_____ Was the speech presented extemporaneously?

_____ Did gestures and body language complement ideas?

_____ Was the speaker's voice expressive?

_____ Did the speaker maintain good eye-contact?

_____ Were notes used unobtrusively?

_____ Were the rate and loudness appropriate to the material?

**Ethics**

_____ Did this speech reveal its actual purpose?

_____ Did the speaker discuss all options?

_____ Would consequences of this speech be desirable?

_____ Are you better for having heard this speech?

*Part III*

---

# CHAPTER-BY-CHAPTER GUIDE

# 1

## Public Speaking as Communication

## CHAPTER OBJECTIVES

After reading Chapter 1, students should be able to:

1. Explain how the skills learned in a public speaking course carry over into everyday interactions.

2. Define the speaker's ethical responsibility and show how different types of speeches can exert control over the listeners.

3. Compare the four characteristics of an ethical speech with the listener's ethical responsibility.

4. Draw, label, and explain the dynamic circle model of communication.

5. Discuss the four components of speaker ethos.

6. Explain the concept of identification in speeches.

7. Identify the three structural parts of a speech and explain the function performed by transitions.

8. Differentiate between abstract and concrete language.

# DISCUSSION (TEXT P. 26)

**1.** Discuss how the ethics of communication might be applied to advertising. Bring to class an example of an advertisement that you think is unethical. Explain why you believe it is unethical.

**Comments:** Focus on

(a) The personal consequences for the reader who sees the advertisement: (1) creation of a need for an unneeded product, (2) support of an addiction such as alcoholism or smoking, (3) encouragement of a false expectation or personal ideal ("If I use this toothpaste, I will have a better love life"), and (4) perpetuation of a stereotypical image of women, men, minorities, or the elderly.

(b) The agenda-setting function of the advertisement—what is suggested as the most important issue for the reader?

(c) How the advertisement might be rated using the four characteristics of an ethical speech: (1) respect for the audience, (2) responsible knowledge of the topic, (3) presentation of accurate and objective information, and (4) concern for the possible consequences of the presentation.

**2.** Whenever there is a revolutionary takeover in a country, usually one of the first things to be controlled by the new government is the means of public communication. Why is this so?

**Comments:** You may examine how media such as radio, television, and public assembly are means of disseminating information that may be unfavorable to a new government. An unstable government may wish to present its opposition from organizing support by censoring public communication. Discussion can then contrast this picture with a look at the United States, where those who oppose the government's policies can freely use any available medium to publicize their efforts.

**3.** What personal and social benefits are lost in societies that do not encourage the free and open exchange of ideas?

**Comments:** Although the class will probably create a longer list, the base list should include the loss of such personal benefits as creativity (for example, the eloquent protest of Russian poets); personal development opportunities; critical listening development; and active decision making. Examples of social benefits lost might include policy decisions arising from full debate, personal freedoms, and an ethical environment.

**4.** Identify speakers you think have high and low ethos. In what areas of ethos are they strong or weak?

**Comments:** Ethos is a very subjective concept. Students from different backgrounds may perceive the same speaker differently. Consider the four dimensions of ethos separately (competence, attractiveness, integrity, and power). Ask students to identify speakers who are high on the competence dimension of ethos and list three such speakers on the chalkboard. Then elicit responses for speakers who are low on the competence dimension. Have students defend their nominations and discuss the differences. Consider the other components of ethos in the same manner.

You can vary this discussion by having the students name a speaker (e.g., Ronald Reagan or Margaret Thatcher) and then discuss a particular speaker in terms of his or her ethos using the four dimensions of ethos. You may want to use a 10-point rating scale for each dimension, with 10 being extremely high and 1 being extremely low. For example, you might get the following results:

| **Ronald Reagan** | | **Richard Nixon** | |
|---|---|---|---|
| Competence | 10 | Competence | 8 |
| Attractiveness | 10 | Attractiveness | 7 |
| Integrity | 8 | Integrity | 3 |
| Power | 10 | Power | 5 |

# APPLICATION (TEXT P. 26)

1. Does your classroom offer a favorable setting for presenting speeches? What kinds of noise might you anticipate in this environment? Develop ideas for handling such interference if it occurs during your presentation.

**Comments:** To help students complete this exercise, you could:

(a) Have students list types of noise and environmental distractions (five minutes).
(b) Put students into groups to discuss and compare their lists, create a master list, and propose a strategy for handling the problems they have listed.
(c) Have each group present an oral report at the end of each class.

Typical classroom environmental distractions include poor acoustics, crowded seating conditions, clutter at the front of the room surrounding the speaker, notes left on the chalkboard, excessive heat or cold, outside noises, people entering the room after class has started, noisy heating or cooling equipment, fire alarms going off.

2. Analyze a speech using the dynamic circle model described in this chapter. Did the source rate well in terms of ethos? Was the idea clear and impressive? Was the mes-

sage well designed? Did the medium pose any problems? Was the audience attentive? How did the listeners respond? Did the communication environment have an effect on the speech? Did the speech change the communication environment? Report your analysis to the class.

**Comments:** (a) Instruct students to select a "live" speech for this exercise—for example, a special lecture on campus, a sermon, or a lecture in another class.

(b) Students should write a report detailing the seven elements of the dynamic circle as they were manifest in the speech. Students should write a brief answer for each question.

(c) This exercise can also be used as the basis of a class discussion or class reports.

(d) Ask each student to report on the element in the speech that he or she considered most interesting.

If the assignment is given prior to class discussion of the dynamic circle elements, the instructor may wish to prepare a model report for the class. I often talk about my consulting experiences in classes, noting how environmental factors like the size of the room affect the message.

**3.** Begin keeping a speech analysis notebook in which you record notes on effective and ineffective speeches you hear both in and out of class. Use the nine criteria for evaluating speeches discussed in this chapter.

**Comments:**

This exercise is useful during the first few weeks of the course while students are beginning to discover the complexity of the speech process. Like any continuing assignment, students will be more diligent if the journals are collected and graded weekly. Set a minimum number of speech entries per week (at least three). As a form of feedback, duplicate the most interesting entries for the class or spend a few minutes each week soliciting verbal comments about what seems to make a speech effective or ineffective.

**4.** Among the speakers presented in Appendix B, Elie Wiesel is noteworthy for his commitment, Ronald Reagan for effectiveness of language use, and Bill Cosby for audience involvement. Study their speeches and make notes about how these qualities are established.

**Comments:** This application item may be used as an in-class exercise or as homework. You might wish to assign the item as a written assignment to be graded and returned for discussion during the next class.

An alternate procedure would be to divide the class into three groups, assigning one of the speeches to each group. The groups would have 30 minutes to prepare a report on their speech and then present these reports to the class. The responses would include the following:

(a) Elie Wiesel (commitment): Note how he supports his speech through personal experience with his autobiographical narrative of the young boy discovering the "kingdom of night." Mention should also be made of the way Mr. Wiesel extends his views to encompass all who are persecuted because of their race, religion, or political views.

(b) Ronald Reagan (effective language use): Observe the parallel construction where Reagan speaks of each of the astronauts: "We remember...." Mention should also be made of Reagan's use of the frontier and family metaphors. He relates the exploration of space to the development of the American frontier and refers to the astronauts as America's sons and daughters.

(c) Bill Cosby (audience involvement): Cosby opens his speech by directly addressing the graduates in the audience, making them feel that he is talking *with* them rather than *to* them. He maintains this directness throughout the speech. His asides about having nothing on underneath the academic gown and passing a bottle around lighten the mood and increase identification. He also includes the parents in the audience by telling the graduates where "forth" is.

# ADDITIONAL EXERCISES

## BENEFITS OF PUBLIC SPEAKING SURVEY

**Purpose:** To check the business advantages of speech training; to provide experience in writing a basic phone script.

**Procedures:**

1. Assign students to work groups.

2. Ask each group to write a script for use in calling local personnel officers or managers (a different firm for each group member). Each script should ask: "How important are speech and listening skills for entry-level management jobs in your business?"

3. Each group should report to the class on (a) their script and (b) the results of the phone survey.

## CLASS CODE OF ETHICS

**Purpose:** To explore the practical ramifications of ethical conduct in the public speaking classroom.

**Procedures:**

1. Divide the class into groups.

2. Assign each group the task of preparing a "Code of Ethics" for the speech class-room—what behaviors and attitudes are or are not ethical in this context?

3. Each group should report its code to the class.

4. Discuss the similarities and differences between the codes.

5. Create a "Class Code of Ethics" from the ideas submitted by the groups.

6. The instructor should duplicate the class code and distribute it to the class. The class code can be used in future discussions when students exhibit use or ignorance of the rules of good conduct.

One item which might appear in the code is: "never enter the room when another student is speaking." Someone will inevitably break this rule, providing a forum for discussion of the consequences of such behavior on both speaker and audience.

## LISTENER CODE OF ETHICS

**Purpose:** To discuss the ethical behaviors of listeners.

**Procedures:**

1. Divide the class into work groups.

2. Ask each group to create an "Ethical Code of Behaviors for Listeners" in the public speaking course.

3. Have each group report its code to the class.

4. Discuss the similarities and differences between the codes.

5. Create a "Class Ethical Code of Behaviors for Listeners." The instructor should duplicate and distribute the code.

One item that might appear in the code is: "listeners should actively pay attention to the speaker rather than be preparing homework for another class." A violation of this rule could provide a forum for discussion of the effects of such behavior on the speaker and the environment of the class.

## ADDITIONAL RESOURCES

Jensen, J. Verson. "Teaching Ethics in Speech Communication." *Communication Education* 34 (October 1985): 324–330.

Johannesen, Richard L. *Ethics in Human Communication*, 2nd ed. (Prospect Heights, Ill.: Waveland Press, 1983).

Johnson, John R., and Nancy Szczupakiewicz. "The Public Speaking Course: Is it Preparing Students with Work Related Public Speaking Skills?" *Communication Education* 36 (April 1987): 131–137.

Kramer, Cheris. "Women's and Men's Ratings of Their Own and Ideal Speech." *Communication Quarterly* 26 (Spring 1978): 2–10.

McFarland, J.L. "The Role of Speech in Self Development, Self-Concept, and Decentration." *Communication Education* 33 (July 1984): 231–236.

Modaff, J., and R. Hopper. "Why Speech Is Basic." *Communication Education* 33 (January 1984): 37–42.

Pearson, Judy C., Ritch L. Sorenson, and Paul E. Nelson. "How Students and Alumni Perceive the Basic Course." *Communication Education* 30 (1981): 296–299.

Sorenson, Ritch L., and Judy C. Pearson. "Alumni Perspectives on Speech Communication Training: Implications for Communication Faculty." *Communication Education* 30 (1981): 299–304.

## SPECIAL FEATURE: CROSSWORD PUZZLE

**Directions:** Complete the crossword puzzle on the following page.

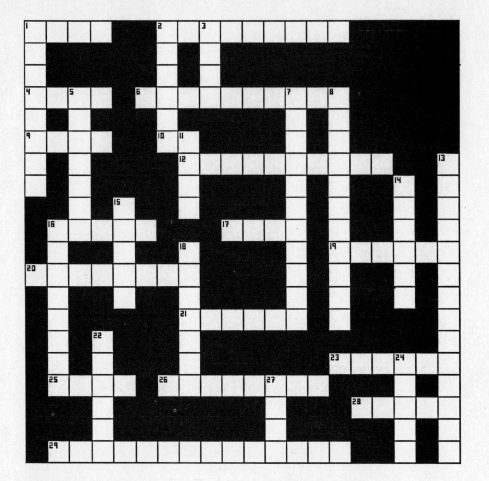

## Across

1. money owed
2. the argument
4. footnote abbreviation
6. a speech type
9. per
10. pronoun
12. a speech type
16. types of evidence
17. brainstorm
19. how message travels
20. audience reaction
21. message originator
23. audience's task
25. Spock's friend
26. audience member
28. beginning of speech
29. audience-speaker tie

## Down

1. act of giving the speech
2. topic of the class
3. prejudice
5. Lee _____
7. a speech type
8. dynamic circle's home
11. reverberation
13. type of presentation
14. speaker responsibility
15. credibility
16. audience response
18. what is transmitted
22. the dynamic _____
24. sum
27. sleeveless garment

## ANSWERS TO CHAPTER 1 PUZZLE

**Across**
1. debt
2. substance
4. ibid
6. persuasive
9. each
10. he
12. ceremonial
16. facts
17. idea
19. medium
20. response
21. source
23. listen
25. Kirk
26. receiver
28. intro
29. identification

**Down**
1. delivery
2. speech
3. bias
5. Iacocca
7. informative
8. environment
11. echo
13. extemporaneous
14. ethics
15. ethos
16. feedback
18. message
22. circle
24. total
27. vest

# 2

---

# Your First Speech

## CHAPTER OBJECTIVES

---

After reading Chapter 2, students should be able to:

1. Identify the four dimensions that determine the listeners' perception of ethos and explain how a speaker can develop or exhibit them.

2. Differentiate between natural power and conferred power.

3. Identify the main parts of a speech.

4. Explain the two purposes of the introduction in a speech.

5. Develop a narrative for an introductory speech.

6. Explain the two purposes of a conclusion.

7. Distinguish between the preparation outline and the key-word outline, and identify the purpose of each.

8. Prepare a preparation outline and a key-word outline.

9. Understand that an improved conversation style is appropriate for public speaking.

10. Use cognitive restructuring to control performance anxiety.

# DISCUSSION (TEXT PP. 52–53)

**1.** While we have defined *ethos* in terms of public speaking, all sources of communication seek to create favorable impressions of competence, integrity, attractiveness, and power. Advertisers especially try to create favorable ethos for their products. Bring to class four print advertisements that emphasize each of the four dimensions of ethos we have discussed. Share them with the class, explaining how each ad uses ethos.

**Comments:** Some suggestions for advertisements include advertisements featuring medical personnel, demonstrating competence; lay testimony advertisements for Tylenol to demonstrate trust or integrity; advertisements featuring athletes or film stars, stressing attractiveness; MasterCard advertisements, focus on power.

**2.** Select a prominent public speaker for ethos analysis. On which dimensions is this speaker stronger? Weaker? How does this affect the person's leadership ability? Present your analysis for class discussion.

**Comments:** For example, Chrysler Corporation's Lee Iacocca is perceived as competent because he took command of a failing company and converted it into a profitable enterprise. He appears honest and dependable (integrity), because he speaks in a straightforward way. He exudes personal qualities that help us to identify with him. He has both conferred power (leadership of a major automobile company) and natural power (a competence and dynamism).

Margaret Thatcher is perceived as competent because, as prime minister of Great Britain, she has led her country through tough economic times. She usually appears to have integrity, although, like most world leaders, occasionally faces criticism in this area. She is an attractive and charming person, in the tradition of British formality. Her conferred power derives from being elected prime minister; her natural power comes from her competence and attractiveness.

**3.** Political advertising often introduces candidates creating favorable ethos for them and sometimes unfavorable ethos for their opponents. Study the television ads in connection with a contemporary election campaign. Bring to class answers to the following questions:

   (a) What kinds of positive and negative identities do the ads establish?
   (b) Which of the inventory questions discussed in this chapter might explain these candidate introductions?
   (c) Which of these ads are most and least effective in creating the desired ethos?

**Comments:** You may wish to videotape three or four advertisements for use in class. Try to find advertisements that introduce candidates new to politics. Discussion should focus on the following areas:

(a) Evaluate the ethos of the candidates in terms of their competence, attractiveness, integrity, and power. Identify script segments and visuals that highlight these factors.

(b) Most of the inventory questions can be found in political advertisements. Politicians are frequently identified as having strong middle-class or working-class backgrounds and coming from rural environments (the "heartland of America"). Experience (especially in a military setting) is often cited, and candidates are generally shown participating in some activity such as walking or playing touch football. Work is usually mentioned to establish the candidates' qualifications for office. Goals and values are often stressed in the advertisements, and the candidates may be pictured with successful and respected associates, such as local political leaders.

(c) Have the class members nominate and vote for the advertisement they believe creates the most effective ethos for its candidate. Each nomination must be explained.

As an alternative, the exercise can be conducted using radio commercials or campaign brochures.

**4.** Identify negative messages you might send yourself concerning public speaking. How might you change these messages, using the principles of cognitive restructuring?

**Comments:** Have students list the three negative messages they most frequently send themselves about public speaking. Then divide the class into groups of three or four students. Each student should share his or her negative messages with the small group and elicit suggestions from group members for changing these messages. Each group should compile a list of negative messages that are sent by more than one member and share these and the recommended changes with the rest of the class.

# APPLICATION (TEXT P. 53)

**1.** As the first speeches are presented in your class, build a collection of portraits of your classmates as revealed by their speeches. At the end of the assignment, analyze this group of portraits to see what you have learned about the class as a whole. What kind of speeches might they prefer? Did you detect any strong political or social attitudes to which you might have to adjust? Submit one copy of your analysis to your instructor and keep another for your own use in preparing later speeches.

**Comments:** Read the analyses, looking for different points of view. Have the students representing these views (perhaps three or four) present them in class, focusing not so much on individual speakers but on the class as a whole. Class discussion should follow, focusing on students' discoveries of common social and political attitudes, areas of obvious interest, and speech topics that seem appropriate for this audience. Together the class should build a composite audience analysis for the purpose of later speech adaptation.

**2.** Using the criteria developed in Chapter 1 for speech evaluation, decide which were the three best speeches presented during the first round of speeches. Write a brief paper defending your choices.

**Comments:** This assignment could also work as a class exercise.

(a) Have students nominate the speeches they thought to be the best.

(b) After several nominations, discuss what each of the nominated speeches had in common to disinguish them from the rest.

During the early portions of the class, you may wish to emphasize that although the class will focus on one concept at a time, an excellent speech delivers on all of the criteria. A speech that is superior in one or two of the following elements can still be a flop if the other elements are neglected.

The nine criteria for an effective speech are speaker commitment, well-chosen topic, clear sense of purpose, audience involvement, substance, appropriate structure, skillful language use, effective presentation, and ethical consequences.

**3.** Select a speech from Appendix B of this book and outline it, using the concepts introduced in this chapter. What principle of design was followed in the speech? Did you detect any structural flaws? Hand in a copy of your outline and your structural analysis to the instructor.

**Comments:** Students may use the following questions to help complete their outline and analysis.

(a) Did the speech have a guiding design or was it disorganized?

(b) Was the design categorical, sequential, cause-effect, spatial, or something else? At this point, students know very little about patterns of design. To prevent frustration, you might introduce the assignment by noting that a speech will have some overall design, and within that design may also have sections based on other design patterns. The student's job is to discover the overall design and how it was implemented.

(c) Did the speech have an introduction that aroused attention and set up the rest of the speech?

(d) Was there a clear thematic statement?

(e) Was the conclusion effective?

## ADDITIONAL EXERCISES

### NARRATIVES

**Purpose:** To practice creating narratives.

**Procedures:**

1. This mini-speech exercise may be an individual or group assignment in class.

2. Ask each student or group to write a narrative to use as the opening of a speech about a travel experience. The narrative should be short, active, and use colorful and concrete language.

3. Have each person (or a representative from each group) deliver the narrative in class.

4. Ask the class to discuss the mini-speeches by focusing on these questions: How well did the narrative arouse interest? How well did the narrative create a context that the audience could identify with? Was it too long or too short? Was the language used colorful, descriptive, concrete, and active?

# PREPARATION OUTLINE WORKSHEET

Topic:

Specific Purpose:

Thematic Statement:

## INTRODUCTION

Attention-getting material:

Establish credibility:

Preview purpose and content:

## BODY

Main point #1:

Subpoints:

Main point #2:

Subpoints:

Main point #3:

Subpoints:

## CONCLUSION

Summary:

Concluding remarks:

## OUTLINING EXERCISE

**Purpose:** To practice outlining prior to the first graded assignment.

**Procedures:**

1. This exercise may be done as an individual homework assignment or as a group assignment in class.

2. Distribute a blank form of the Preparation Outline Worksheet, page 42.

3. Ask each student or group to create a preparation outline on one of the following topics:
   • Registering for classes
   • Finding a parking place on campus
   • Living with roommates
   • The day I left for college

If this is a group assignment, you may wish to have each group work on a different topic.

4. Discuss with the class which portions of the speech should be outlined first (thematic statement, body, introduction, or conclusion).

5. Grade each outline for its strengths and weaknesses: Is the thematic statement clear? Does the content deliver on the theme suggested by the thematic statement? Are the main points developed sufficiently? Does the introduction generate interest? Write specific suggestions for improvements on each outline. Comment on what was done well and what needed improvement. If the exercise is done as a group assignment, duplicate the outlines and your comments. Distribute the marked-up outlines to the class as models of what you expect future outlines to include. (You may want to mask the grades on any materials you duplicate for the class.)

## ADDITIONAL RESOURCES

Ayers, Joe. "Perceptions of Speaking Ability: An Explanation for Stage Fright." *Communication Education* 35 (July 1986): 275–287.

Hufman, Melody. "The Maze as an Instructional Instrument for Public Speaking." *Communication Education* 34 (January 1985): 63–68.

Johnson, Craig E. "An Introduction to Powerful and Powerless Talk in the Classroom." *Communication Education* 36 (April 1987): 167–172.

Littlefield, Robert S., and Timothy L. Sellnow. "The Use of Self-Disclosure as a Means for Reducing Stage-Fright in Beginning Speakers." *Communication Education* 36 (January 1987): 62–64.

"Stagefright." A Centron Film (videotape). 13 minutes. Coronet/MTI Film and Video Co.

# 3

# Critical Listening and Speech Evaluation

## CHAPTER OBJECTIVES

After reading Chapter 3, students should be able to:

1. Explain why listening is essential to the dynamic circle of communication.

2. Distinguish between hearing and critical listening, and discuss several areas where critical listening is essential.

3. Identify and discuss the sources of listening problems.

4. Differentiate between the denotative and the connotative meaning of a word.

5. Identify poor listening habits and the steps toward more effective listening.

6. Explain how trigger words can block critical listening.

7. Explain the differences between critiquing a speech and criticizing a speaker.

8. Apply the nine general guidelines to evaluate speeches.

# DISCUSSION (TEXT P. 77)

**1.** Complete the listening self-analysis checklist on page 67 in Chapter 3 of the text. Working in groups of five, share your listening problems with the other members of the group. Develop a listening improvement plan for the three most common listening problems in your group. Report this plan to the rest of the class.

**Comments:** Students' plans to improve listening will vary widely. Some items on the checklist describe a self-awareness level, where increased self-awareness is the first necessary step to improvement (1, 13). A number of items relate to the listener's accepting responsibility for part of the communication process (2, 5, 6, 8, 9, 14, 15, 16, 19). Other items refer to the listener's skill problems (17, 18). Still other items refer to attitude barriers in the listener (3, 4, 7, 10, 11, 12, 20). The instructor should help students to recognize that the recommended solutions must be relevant to the types of problems.

**2.** List three positive and three negative trigger words that arouse a strong emotional reaction when you hear them. One person should serve as a recorder to write these words on the chalkboard. Try to group the words into categories, such as sexist or ethnic slurs, political terms, ideal words, etc. Discuss why these words have such a potent impact for you. Do you feel your reactions to them are justified?

**Comments:** You may wish to share three personal examples when assigning the task. Trigger words for me are *unfair* (teachers hate to be thought of as unfair), *girl* (part of my consciousness-raising training), and *political mandate* (just because many people vote for someone doesn't mean they all endorse a specific policy). My reactions to these trigger words vary. Becoming defensive is one reaction. Discussion should focus on how, as consumers of information, we should learn our trigger words so that we can put rationality back into the communication process and not be short-circuited or side-tracked whenever we hear them.

Further discussion could focus on whether or not it is ethical for speakers to use known trigger words.

**3.** From among the classes you are now taking (excluding this class), select the teacher you feel presents the best lectures. Evaluate that teacher's communication skills using the guide on pages 70–71 in Chapter 3 of the text. Which of these criteria influenced your evaluation the most? Share your evaluation with your class in discussion.

**Comments:** This exercise gives you an opportunity to encourage specific, concrete, and precise evaluative comments, rather than the vague, generic comments students usually offer. When processing the exercise within the class, you may want to probe the students whenever they give generic evaluations. For example, you might say, "What *exactly* is it about Dr. Smith's lectures that gives you the impression that he is committed?" Students should be encouraged not to use teachers' real names in order to avoid debates between class members or hurt feelings.

# APPLICATION (TEST PP. 77–78)

**1.** Review the notes you have taken in one of your lecture courses. Are you able to identify the main points, or have you been trying to write down everything that was said? Compare your note-taking before and after studying listening behavior. Can you see any difference?

**Comments:** Students' assessment of their note-taking will vary. To help them compare note-taking before and after studying Chapter 3 of the text, you might suggest that students create two outlines, from two separate sets of lecture notes. Each outline should be based on a different lecture, one that preceded the study of listening behavior and one that followed it. Which outline includes the main points and the subpoints developed under each main idea? Is one outline more succinct and easier to study from?

Students who cannot see any difference in their before and after outlines (or notes) might try the following exercise. This exercise directs students' attention to the nonverbal cues of the speaker to determine what is important. The exercise needs to be done during a lecture in another class. During the lecture, if the instructor raises his or her voice or puts other vocal stress on a concept, have students put a star beside it in their notes. If the instructor repeats the concept, have students give it another star. If the instructor writes it on the board, have students give the concept a third star. Any additional stress on a concept warrants an additional star beside it in their notes. The odds are good that many test questions will be written from starred material—the more stars, the greater the probability that a concept is important enough to become a test item.

**2.** Do you have any friends who are poor listeners? Describe their behavior to the class and make specific recommendations for their improvement.

**Comments:** This exercise can be assigned to groups in class. Divide the class into work groups and have every member of each group work silently for three minutes to write down the behaviors of a friend who listens poorly. After the independent work, have each member share the description with his or her group. Once each member has shared, instruct each group to select one example to be role-played for the class. One group member will play the speaker who is sharing some important information. The group member who contributed the selected description will play the friend who is a poor listener. A pair from each group will role-play the speaker-listener interaction.

Discussion can focus on: What listening problems are illustrated in each scene? How do you feel when someone doesn't listen? How can we help our friends to be better listeners? Can we alert poor listeners to their habits by making caring but assertive statements such as, "This is really important to me; I wish you would look like you're listening"?

**3.** Prepare a critique of a prominent political or religious speaker. What positive and constructive advice would you offer this person?

**Comments:** The critique should be done on a live or televised speech, using the evaluation form on pages 70 and 71 of the text. The advice offered should directly relate to the criteria enumerated on the evaluation form.

To add spice to the exercise, ask that the constructive advice portion be written in the form of a letter to the speaker. The letter should include a reference to the occasion when the student heard the speaker; comments on the speaker's strengths, weaknesses, and ability to identify with and involve the audience; and recommendations for improvement of subsequent speeches.

This exercise gives you an opportunity to encourage concrete, specific evaluation, rather than the generic, vague criticism students often offer. Probe any generic comments to discover the specific underlying reasons for students' opinions.

**4.** Evaluate a contemporary speaker on ethical grounds. Be sure to distinguish between ethical uses of speech techniques and the moral consequences of messages. Be prepared to present and defend your judgments in class.

**Comments:** Students should use the criteria in the evaluation form (page 71 of the text) and ethics discussion of Chapter 3 as guidelines. You may wish to focus class discussion of individual speakers, and their speeches, on the four criteria in the evaluation form:

(a) *Did this speech reveal its actual purpose?* What speech did you hear that revealed its actual purpose? What speeches did you hear that concealed their actual purposes? Why do you think the speaker chose to reveal or conceal his or her actual purposes? How did you feel when you discovered afterward what the real purpose of the speech was? Would you call the act of not revealing the actual purpose unethical in these cases?

(b) *Did the speaker discuss all options?* What speeches did you hear that discussed both sides of an issue? What speeches did you hear that discussed only one side of an issue? Would you consider the cases where only one option was presented unethical?

(c) *Would the consequences of this speech be desirable?* What are the possible good consequences of speeches you heard? What are the possible bad consequences of speeches you heard? Would you call the consequences unethical? How bad does a consequence have to be before it becomes unethical? What about consequences that are a surprise to the speaker?

(d) *Are you better for having heard this speech?* If you are not better, does that make it unethical?

Find areas of agreement on conditions that are clearly unethical (the speaker knowingly lies to the audience). Find areas where students disagree. For example, many critics call President Reagan's mistakes in presenting information in press conferences unethical because he passes incorrect or conflicting information to the public. Others say it is not unethical because his intent is good, even though the implementation may sometimes be poor. Where do we draw the line?

# ADDITIONAL EXERCISES

## LISTENING INVENTORY

**Purpose:** To discover the distractions in the classroom area.

**Procedure:**

1. Tell students to remain silent for five minutes while they write down all the sounds they hear in the classroom.

2. Make a list on the board of all the distractions discovered.

3. Discuss what sounds were heard. How distracting would these sounds be for speakers and listeners? What can speakers and listeners do to minimize these distractions?

An interesting variation of this exercise is to select a day when you are lecturing and instruct the first five to ten students who arrive for class to do a listening inventory that day. Use the last five minutes of class to discuss the distractions these students itemize.

## AUDIENCE LISTENING PROFILE

**Purpose:** To become aware of audience listening habits.

**Procedures:**

1. Instruct students to complete this assignment: In a listening situation other than this class, observe the audience's listening behaviors. Write down examples of good and poor listening behaviors. What is the level of listening behavior common to most of the audience? Prepare a written report.

2. In class, discuss the types of good listening behaviors and poor listening habits observed. Relate the discussion to the 25-percent retention rate of the average adult listener. Make sure the discussion covers the types of listening problems presented in the text.

## LISTENING FOR CONTENT

**Purpose:** To practice listening for the main ideas; to practice forming questions of clarification.

**Procedures:**

1. Invite a member of your local forensics team to present a speech to the class on a controversial topic. If a speech team member is not available, you can play a tape or read a transcript of a controversial speech.

2. Instruct students to take notes on the main points of the speech, marking their notes at places where they may wish to ask questions of clarification.

3. After the speech has been presented, instruct students to form questions of clarification about the speech to check their understanding of the content.

4. Have students present their questions. Be sure the questions are questions of clarification, rather than rebuttals.

5. Then discuss some of the following questions: How difficult is it to listen to a controversial topic? Did you discover any trigger words during the speech? Did outlining the speech help you maintain your attention? Did marking your notes for places to ask questions of clarification help? Did you fall victim to any of the bad listening practices listed in the chapter?

6. Have students write a paragraph on their reactions to the speech as listeners and what they can do to be better listeners in situations where the topic is controversial.

# ADDITIONAL RESOURCES

Arnett, R.C., and G. Nakagawa. "The Assumptive Roots of Empathic Listening: A Critique." *Communication Education* 32 (October 1983): 368–378.

Boileau, Don M. "Listening: Teaching and Research." *Communication Education* 32 (October 1983): 441–447.

Bostrom, Robert N., and Carol L. Bryant. "Factors in the Retention of Information Presented Orally: The Role of Short-Term Listening." *Western Journal of Speech Communication* 44 (Spring 1980): 137–145.

Floyd, James J. *Listening: A Practical Approach.* (Glenview, Ill.: Scott, Foresman and Co., 1985).

Galvin, Kathleen. *Listening by Doing.* (Lincolnwood, Ill.: National Textbook Co., 1985).

Glatthorn, Allan A., and Herbert R. Adams. *Listening Your Way to Management Success.* (Glenview, Ill.: Scott, Foresman and Co., 1983).

Rubin, Rebecca B. "Assessing Speaking and Listening Competence at the College Level: The Communication Competency Assessment Instrument." *Communication Education* 31 (January 1982): 19–32.

Wolf, Florence I., et al. *Perceptive Listening.* (New York, N.Y.: Holt, Rinehart and Winston, 1983).

Wolvin, Andrew D., and Carolyn Gwynn Coakley. *Listening*, 2nd ed. (Dubuque, Iowa: Wm. C. Brown, 1985).

"Listening." Roundtable, 1972. 17 minutes.

"Listening and Speaking." Films for the Humanities. 15 minutes.

"Many Hear–Some Listen." Centron Film (videotape). 12 minutes. Coronet/MTI Film and Video Co.

"The Power of Listening." CRM/McGraw-Hill. 26 minutes.

"Receiving a Message." Films for the Humanities. 15 minutes.

## SPECIAL FEATURE: CROSSWORD PUZZLE

Directions: Complete the crossword puzzle on the following page.

## Across

1. investment in speech in terms of intensity and research

3. intent of speech
6. short entry in newspaper
7. solid object with six square sides
8. one criterion for speech evaluation
9. before Easter
10. listeners
12. oral or written _____
13. _____ persuaders
14. type of language that suggests attitudes or emotions
16. removal of bias
19. don't criticize, _____
20. smells offensive

## Down

1. _____ listening

2. subject of speech
3. overall delivery
4. message supported by evidence
5. organized, clear design
11. type of meaning that is dictionary definition
12. personal record of class speeches
15. intense words that block listening

17. not fronts
18. small bed

# ANSWERS TO CHAPTER 3 PUZZLE

**Across**
1. commitment
3. purpose
6. item
7. cube
8. ethics
9. Lent
10. audience
12. language
13. hidden
14. connotative
16. objectivity
19. critique
20. reeks

**Down**
1. critical
2. topic
3. presentation
4. substance
5. structure
11. denotative
12. log
15. trigger
17. backs
18. cot

# 4

---

# Selecting and Researching Your Topic

## CHAPTER OBJECTIVES

---

After reading Chapter 4, students should be able to:

1. Understand the four characteristics of a good speech topic.

2. Work through the four stages of a topic search.

3. Know how to use the popular media as a source of speech topics.

4. Use the six-question method of topic analysis to frame a specific topic for an informative or a persuasive speech.

5. Determine a general and a specific purpose for a speech topic.

6. Develop a thematic statement.

7. Make appropriate use of personal experience to add credibility and authenticity to a speech.

8. Identify the five characteristics of responsible knowledge of a topic.

9. Obtain information from the major research resources found in most libraries.

10. Design and conduct an information-seeking interview, using probes, mirror questions, verifiers, and reinforcers.

11. Prepare the two major kinds of research note cards--information cards and source cards.

## DISCUSSION (TEXT P. 110)

1. Bring a chart of your interests to class and exchange it with classmates. Discuss the most promising areas for speech topics among your interests.

**Comments:** you can assign the chart as homework. Have students complete an interest chart like Figure 4.1 (on page 85 of the text), including at least five elements under each category. In work groups during class, students can exchange their charts and look for common areas of interest under each heading.

Discussion can focus on questions such as: Were you surprised by the number of similarities or differences in your group? Did this exercise help you gain insights into finding topic areas for different audiences?

2. Analyze in class the most promising topic areas discovered in the previous discussion, using the topic analysis method. As you identify topic possibilities, consider what general purposes they might serve.

**Comments:** Using the same groups as for Discussion Question 1, have each group select one area to analyze as a possible topic. Then select one person to record the list of topic areas for the class. Brainstorm the topic areas, using the "who, what, when, where, why, and how" method described in the chapter. After you have brainstormed the possible areas, classify them according to general purpose: to inform, persuade, entertain, or celebrate.

3. As a follow-up to Questions 1 and 2, develop specific purposes and thematic statements for the three topics that interest you most. Evaluate them in class, using the methods for selecting good topics and determining specific purposes described in this chapter.

**Comments:** Instruct students to quickly choose three topic areas from the list developed in Question 2. Students should then formulate a specific purpose for their first choice, applying the questions in the chapter to test the appropriateness of the specific purpose. Have students repeat this process for their other two topics.

Class discussion of selected topics can include such questions as: Are you surprised by the changes in focus in your topic from the initial idea to the specific purpose? How valuable is this process in helping you frame a topic? What would happen if you accepted the first topic that came to mind rather than going through all the steps in the process?

**4.** In what ways might personal experience limit and distort your knowledge as well as enrich it? Discuss in class in terms of your own experience.

**Comments:** Generally personal experience can limit knowledge by creating: (a) bias or tunnel vision on a particular topic, (b) overconfidence in one's knowledge of a topic, which can be overcome by verifying facts through research or interviews, (c) use of "insider's" language, jargon that makes sense to the speaker but is unknown to the audience, and (d) lack of clarity (knowing how to do something is different from knowing how to explain how to do something). During the class discussion, list on the board the advantages and disadvantages suggested by students. Discuss how awareness of the limiting factors and good management can turn disadvantages into advantages.

# APPLICATION (TEXT PP. 110–111)

**1.** Working in teams of five students, scan print media to generate topic areas for speeches. Each team should be responsible for checking one of the following resources:

a. the local Sunday newspaper

b. a television news program over a week's time

c. a recent issue of a weekly news magazine

d. a recent issue of a general-interest magazine such as *Saturday Evening Post*

e. the campus newspaper from the previous week

In the first part of a class period, meet as teams to generate a list of topic ideas suggested by your scanning. Each team should select five topic ideas on the basis of general interest and appropriateness to a speech assignment. In the second part of the class period, a representative of each group should present team recommendations to the class as a whole and explain how and why the topics were chosen. Which kind of media resource produces the best speech topics? What are the strengths and limitations of each resource?

Comments: To scan print media, you could assign a specific resource to each group. The groups could then conduct their scans prior to the class session when the rest of the application is to take place. To ensure equal participation, you may want to announce that you will collect a list from each student as homework. The purpose of the exercise is to show that topics are literally everywhere. In the class discussion, give positive feedback to reinforce the idea that good topic areas are easy to find. If students present poor or vague topic areas, help to refine them into more appropriate ideas. When processing the last two questions about which sources are best, reinforce the idea that whether or not sources are useful depends on what you are looking for and whom you will be speaking to (that is, there are no inherently bad sources for topic areas).

**2.** Choose one of the topics you selected for Application 1 and identify the most likely sources of information you could use to develop it.

**Comments:** Using the sources described in the chapter, have students state where they would begin and the specific sources they would consult.

This exercise is a chance to confront the tendency of beginning researchers to use only books and the *Reader's Guide* as sources of information. If time permits, send the class to the library to find what information is available on their topics. Be sure they consult at least five different types of library research resources.

**3.** Based on the speech analysis notebook you are keeping of speeches in class (Application 2, Chapter 1) and the overall analysis you perform after the first round of speeches (Application 1, Chapter 2), identify topics likely to interest your class in the next round of speeches.

**Comments:** Assign students to bring their speech analysis notebooks and overall analysis of the first round of speeches to class on the day you plan to use this exercise. In identifying topics, ask students for more specific information about what aspects of the topic area seem particularly appropriate to the class.

This exercise can work as an individual homework assignment or as a task for work groups. Answers can be discussed in class.

**4.** Take a walking tour of your library and locate the various resources described in this chapter. While you are there, find answers for the following questions. Record the source of each answer.

   a. Who is the world's wealthiest woman and how wealthy is she?

   b. From what play comes the quote "A horse! A horse! My kingdom for a horse!"?

   c. What was the name of Bill Cosby's first television series?

   d. Who is the conductor of the Pittsburgh Philharmonic Orchestra?

   e. What CBS prime-time line-up was pre-empted on November 22, 1963? By what event was it interrupted?

   f. Who were the goalies in the America vs. Russia Olympic gold-medal hockey game in 1980?

g. Which movie won the Academy Award for best picture in 1982?

h. How many seas are named after a color, and what are they?

i. Who said "Old soldiers never die, they just fade away," and where was it said?

j. What is the life expectancy for infants born this year in the United States, and how does this compare with 50 years ago?

k. How many grizzly bears are still alive in the United States?

**Comments:** You may want to do this as two separate assignments: (1) to find the sources listed in the chapter and (2) to answer the trivia questions. If you ask a reference librarian for help with the trivia questions, submit a list of the questions a week in advance so that the librarian can verify that the sources of information are available (not in storage or at the bindery). This courtesy may also secure a list of up-to-date answers.

**5.** Evaluate the information in one of the student speeches in Appendix B of this book in terms of reliability, thoroughness, timeliness, and precision. Based on these criteria alone, what grade would you give the speech?

**Comments:** Be sure students evaluate the information based on what was known at the time of the speech, not new knowledge since the speech's delivery. In their evaluation, students should list where they looked to verify the information. (Inability to know where to look to verify information because the speaker did not give sufficient information *is* a valid reason to grade it low.)

# ADDITIONAL EXERCISES

## PLAG-A-WHAT?

**Purpose:** To define plagiarism and the purpose of documentation.

**Procedures:**

1. Divide the class into work groups. Ask each group to answer one of the following questions through library research or an interview. Students must properly document their sources of information.

a. What is the general definition of plagiarism?

b. What are the university regulations concerning plagiarism?

   **c.** When should written documentation be supplied for information you take from another source? When should verbal documentation be supplied for similar information when you use it in speeches?

   **d.** What are the penalties for copyright violations?

   **e.** What is the speech/communication department's policy on plagiarism?

**Answers:**

   **a.** According to *The American Heritage Dictionary:* the act of stealing and using (the ideas or writings of another) as one's own.

   **b.** Check the student handbook, official handbook of university rules and regulations, university grievance boards, or registrar's office.

   **c.** Whenever you use another's words or ideas, whether directly quoting the source, paraphrasing, or using an original idea. The same documentation applies in speeches—give enough information to listeners can find the source if they wish.

   **d.** Check with the university's lawyer, copyright office, journalism professors, or library reference room.

   **e.** Check with the department chairperson.

   2. Have each group submit both an oral and a written report.

   3. Discuss with students if the rules are too strenuous or too easy. Ask students why a university feels so strongly about plagiarism.

## FORBIDDEN TOPICS LIST

**Purpose:** To discover overused topics.

**Procedures:**

   1. Divide students into work groups. Instruct each group to make a list of topics (a) of which the basics are common knowledge or (b) that have become overused and stale. You may wish to give examples of topics from past classes: popping popcorn, waxing skis, brushing teeth, and so on.

   2. Have each group write their list on the chalkboard.

   3. Discuss: Are there any topics that don't seem to fit the assignment? For the remaining topics, how can we alter them to make them fresher? You may wish to offer some sample answers: "What makes popcorn pop?" instead of "How to pop popcorn"; "Why we use different waxes on different types of snow?" instead of "How to wax a ski."

## NARROWING TOPICS: FOLLOW-UP TO APPLICATION 1

**Purpose:** To practice narrowing topics to fit a limited time frame

**Procedures:**

1. Using the topics generated in Application 1 of this chapter, ask students to narrow the broad topic areas to specific aspects that can be covered in brief speeches (4-6 minutes).

   If the class has not generated topics using Application 1, you can bring a recent newspaper to class and excerpt broad topic areas from it for the class. As another alternative, you can give each group two of the following general areas to narrow.
   • War
   • Light
   • Television music programs
   • Gardening
   • Fire
   • Soda
   • Art
   • Seat belts
   • Exercise
   • Native Americans
   • Coffee
   • Books

2. Have each group present one topic area and discuss how they narrowed it. If the reported topic remains vague or broad, you can help the group narrow it.

## FROM VAGUE TO SPECIFIC PURPOSE

**Purpose:** To practice refining specific purposes

**Procedures:**

1. Review with students that a specific purpose is the controlling idea of a speech. It is written in a clear, declarative form and specifically describes what the audience will know after hearing a speech. Questions to judge a specific purpose include:
   • Do I know enough, or can I learn enough to satisfy my specific purpose?
   • Is the specific purpose important enough to deserve attention?
   • Does this specific purpose offer something new?
   • Is the specific purpose too ambitious?
   • Can I fulfill my specific purpose in the time allocated to me?

2. Assign students to work groups. Give each group the following list of seven vague purposes.

a. To inform the audience how to brush their teeth

b. To inform the audience how to pop popcorn

c. To inform the audience about nuclear physics

d. To inform the audience about indoor and outdoor gardening

e. To persuade the audience to boycott our stupid graduation ceremony

f. To inform the audience about horses

g. To inform the audience how to register for classes

3. Ask each group to diagnose what is wrong with each specific purpose and to redefine it into a better, more narrow specific purpose.

**Answers:**

a. The topic is old, stale, and does not deserve additional attention. A better topic is: to inform the audience how high technology is used to produce new and better toothbrushes.

b. It is not worthy of deeper attention, as everyone probably has mastered this simple task. A better topic is: to inform the audience why popcorn pops.

c. The speaker may not know enough to be credible on the topic. It is too ambitious and needs to be narrowed. A better topic is: to inform the audience about what happens when atoms split.

d. The topic is really two topics and both can be narrowed further. A better topic is: to inform the audience how to force bulbs indoors for winter blooms.

e. The phrasing is offensive and begs the question. A specific purpose should be more objective. Omitting the word "stupid" makes it less offensive.

f. The topic is vague and overly ambitious. A better topic is: to inform the audience about two breeds of horses used in circus performances.

g. The audience probably knows as much about it as the speaker. A topic must offer something fresh to be worthwhile. A better topic is: to inform the audience about three secret ways to a painless registration.

## ADDITIONAL RESOURCES

Baker, Robert K. *Doing Library Research: An Introduction for Community College Students*. (Boulder, Colo.: Westview, 1981).

Douglas, Jack D. *Creative Interviewing*. (Beverly Hills, Calif.: Sage Publications, 1985).

Horowitz, Lois. *Knowing Where to Look: The Ultimate Guide to Research*. (Cincinnati, Ohio: Writer's Digest Books, 1984).

Hunt, Gary, and William Eadie. *Interviewing: A Communication Approach*. (New York, N.Y.: Holt, Rinehart and Winston, 1987).

Stewart, Charles J., and William B. Cash. *Interviewing: Principles and Practices*, 4th ed. (Dubuque, Iowa: Wm. C. Brown, 1985).

"Learning from Others." Films for the Humanities, 1982. 15 minutes.

"Speakers and the Library." Films for the Humanities, 1982. 15 minutes.

"The Topic and the Audience." Films for the Humanities, 1982. 15 minutes.

# 5

## Audience Analysis and Adaptation

## CHAPTER OBJECTIVES

After reading Chapter 5, students should be able to:

1. Explain why audience analysis is an essential component of the public speaking process.

2. Describe major external factors of the communication environment and how speakers should adapt to them.

3. Know how to gather and use demographic data.

4. Distinguish between stereotypes and appropriate inferences based on demographic information.

5. Define and identify sexist language and trigger words.

6. Explain Abraham Maslow's hierarchy of needs and now these five needs may be used as appeals in speeches.

7. Use appeals based on audience's needs and motivations to adapt a message.

8. Differentiate between attitudes and values and belief systems.

# DISCUSSION (TEXT P. 139)

**1.** How might the following situations affect a speech you are about to give? How would you adapt?

**Comments:** A variety of responses are correct. In using this exercise, help students to be sensitive to the needs of the audience and occasion, and also to recognize that not all speakers are alike--all can't use humor to alleviate tension, for example.

a. You are the last speaker during the last class period before the Thanksgiving holiday begins.

**Comments:** The audience is probably eager to leave the campus. A more upbeat speech, using high energy or dramatic appeal, will be necessary to sustain attention. If possible, select a timely topic--the traditions of the holiday or traditional Thanksgiving recreations.

b. A lost student walks into the class right in the middle of your speech, looks around, says "Excuse me," and walks out.

**Comments:** The flow is broken and an awkwardness is created. Composure is the key. Some speakers will prefer to pause during the distraction and then go on. Others will prefer to interact with the intruder by saying something like "No problem" and then continue with the speech.

c. The speaker right before you gives an incredibly successful speech, which brings spontaneous applause from the class and high praise from the instructor.

**Comments:** There are two ways to look at this situation. One is that the audience will have high expectations of the next speaker, who may not be as skilled. The second perspective is to realize that the audience will be awake and alert, primed to listen to whatever the next speaker has to offer. It is important to take advantage of the second view, rather than to be intimidated by the previous speaker's skill. Some speakers may wish to acknowledge the success of the previous speaker during their introduction: "I'm glad Joan did such a good job. I can see that you are all alert and having a good time. That's good, because I have some very important information to share with you today."

d. The speaker right before you bombs badly. Her speech is poorly prepared, she is very nervous, and she simply stops in the middle and sits down, visibly upset.

**Comments:** This situation is uncomfortable for the audience. The audience is tense, yet eager for someone to succeed and dispel the negative mood. By doing your best and maintaining your composure, you can help the audience move beyond the awkwardness of the moment.

e. (It rarely happens, but . . .) The speaker right before you gives a speech on the same topic, taking the same general approach.

**Comments:** The audience has already been informed/persuaded on the topic. They are therefore a different audience for you than for the previous speaker. It is best to make a few quick adjustments to recognize the last speaker, using phrases such as "As you heard earlier" or "I want to reemphasize." Use the previous speaker's speech as the framework for your own, telling the audience that they are fortunate to hear two messages on this important topic. A more experienced speaker may drop entire sections of his or her speech and substitute impromptu information that does not duplicate the previous speaker. Inexperienced speakers should adapt by altering how they introduce their material and by referring to the previous speaker; they should not, however, change their basic speech plan.

**2.** Bring to class an example of an advertisement that exemplifies sexual stereotyping or the use of sexist language. Discuss why such techniques might be used and who the intended audience is. In your opinion, what is the actual effect? Is the ad successful?

**Comments:** Remind students not to tear pages out of library magazines but to copy the advertisements. Sexist techniques are used for both men and women. Some female sexist techniques are used to reinforce women's images of themselves; others are used to draw the attention of men. Likewise, male sexist advertisements are used to reinforce stereotypical images of men or to draw the attention of women. The techniques are used to draw attention or to appeal to our needs for belongingness, sex, esteem, social approval, and so on. Whether or not the advertisements appeal to particular individuals in the class, these types of advertisements are often quite successful.

**3.** Discuss in class how the eight human needs covered in this chapter might make you susceptible to certain speech topics and approaches. Rank these needs in terms of how powerful they are as motivators for you.

**Comments:** The needs are physiological, safety and security, belongingness, esteem, self-actualization, change, independence, and dominance.

This exercise could be done by groups or by the class as a whole. Discuss one need at a time. What kinds of situations create a need in this area? When would you be the most sensitive to these appeals? After discussing each need, ask students to write down the top four needs in their lives now. (You don't need to collect the lists.) Discuss how knowing our need vulnerabilities affects how we listen to speeches or advertisements?

**4.** Construct a hypothetical person who represents the average student at your college or university in terms of age, sex, educational background, group affiliations, and sociocultural background. What speech topics would this hypothetical person find most interesting? What motives, values, and attitudes would this person bring to these topics as a member of the audience? Discuss in class.

**Comments:** This exercise can be done as a group assignment. Divide the class into groups and ask each group to conduct research prior to the next class (registrar's office, university documents, president's office). Instruct each group to use this research to create a list of at least five speech topics for the hypothetical person, based on motives, values, and attitudes. Have each group present their findings in class.

Depending on your university profile, there will be more or less homogeneity. Students should be able to research the demographic profile of the average student. Motives, values, and attitudes will be affected by the profile, geographic location, and other features unique to your school.

## APPLICATION (TEXT PP. 139–141)

**1.** Explain how you would tailor a speech on the general topic of food for an audience of:

a. high school sophomores

b. senior citizens

c. hospital dieticians

d. football players

**Comments:** This exercise works well as a take-home assignment (that will be discussed later in class) or as an in-class assignment. If it is used in class, either groups (of three to five students) or the class as a whole can discuss the responses.

Beginning students often forget to conduct an audience analysis and go directly to tailoring the content of the speech. Therefore the instructor should discuss with the class what one needs to know before tailoring a speech (audience analysis).

The audience-analysis discussion should include the following questions:

• What inferences are you making about the audience? What are their demographics?

• Are the inferences appropriate or stereotypical views of the audience?

• How much would you expect this audience to know about a general food topic? What aspects of nutrition might they be particularly interested in?

• Would this audience have any special motivational needs related to food or nutrition? (Consider Maslow's hierarchy or the other three needs discussed in the chapter.)

• Would this audience have any strong values related to food or nutrition?

After conducting an audience analysis on each of the four suggested audiences, discuss how you would tailor the speech for each. Discussion could include some of the following questions:

•What aspect of food would you choose to talk about? Why is that topic better for the audience than other topics?

• What motivational appeals might you use to evoke interest in your speech?

• What values might you address to evoke interest in your speech?

**2.** Using the general topic of food, provide hypothetical examples you might use based on the following needs:

a. physiological needs

b. belongingness needs

c. need for change

d. need for independence

**Comments:** This exercise works well as a take-home assignment (that will be discussed later in class) or as an in-class assignment. If it is used in class, either the class as a whole or groups (of three to five students) can discuss the responses. This assignment works best if the examples are put in the context of an audience. You could use the audiences in Application 1.

Discussion of physiological needs might focus on:
• What are physiological needs?
• Are the physiological needs the same for the four audiences listed in Application 1? If not, how are they different?
• State an example tailored to each of the four audiences that would appeal to their physiological needs. How are the examples different?
• Are the examples relying on appropriate inferences about the audience rather than stereotyping?

Continue with the same series of questions for each of the remaining three needs in Application 2.

**3.** You have been invited to speak before the Futures Club of your city. Using the topics in this chapter as a checklist, you construct the following picture of the audience you can anticipate in your speech. In light of this picture, what will be your topic and purpose and what major strategies will you follow in your speech?

a. *Speech occasion:* The occasion will be a weekly meeting of the Futures Club, a group of business persons interested in forecasting future trends and encouraging those that seem most beneficial to the community. The meeting consists of a luncheon, an officer's report, and your speech, in that order. You should plan for a 15-minute presentation.

There will be a time for questions and discussion following your speech. The luncheon will be held in a large dining room of a downtown hotel. A speaker's lectern will be provided, and distractions should be minimal. There should be 50 to 60 people in attendance.

At the meeting before your speech, the Futures Club heard an advocate of gray rights urge reforms that will help older Americans. Before that, they heard a state senator present an agenda for major legislation in the next decade. They should be especially interested in your view as a student of what should be conserved and what should be changed in the future. However, you are free to select your own topic and frame your own purpose.

b. *Demographics:* The typical Futures Club member is thirty-five years old, a highly successful, rapidly rising executive in a local firm. Membership is 60 percent male, 40 percent female. The typical member is a college graduate. Many graduated with honors, and a few have advanced degrees. The members are "joiners"—many are boating, golf, and tennis enthusiasts, and belong to various clubs promoting these interests. Republicans outnumber Democrats 2 to 1. Religious commitments are not especially intense: if there is any preferred faith, it is Episcopalian. Most of the members come from white, upper-middle-class families in which they were expected to succeed. A few have rebelled against this background, and are tolerated in the club as a kind of maverick element. The club has five or six black members. Three years ago members realized (with some embarrassment) that they had no Asian or Hispanic members. These ethnic groups are now represented.

c. *Dynamics:* Economically, the club members are well off, although their marriages are often unstable. They have intense needs for belonging, esteem, and self-actualization. The Futures Club itself helps to satisfy these needs. They do not fear change, and they have powerful impulses toward dominance and independence. Their attitudes and values are flexible and somewhat pragmatic: they value programs that produce measurable results. At their best, they want to see qualitative improvements in the life of the community, and they want to feel a part of a positive movement toward such change.

**Comments:** This exercise works well as a take-home assignment that is later used as the basis of a class discussion. Some steps to follow include:

(a) Have each person report his or her topic and purpose.

(b) Discuss the similarities and differences in topics/purposes that were selected.

(c) Categorize topics/purposes on the chalkboard under "Very Appropriate" and "Somewhat Appropriate." Discuss with students the differences in the listings and how appropriateness was determined.

(d) Ask for major strategies that students decided to follow, and list them on the board.

(e) Discuss how the strategies were selected: What in the audience analysis helped students select their strategies?

2. Grading hint: Since the assignment falls relatively early in the term, you may wish to focus grading on the quality of the audience analysis, rather than on the quality of the oral delivery.

3. After all the reports have been completed, discuss: What sources did you use for information on the audience, or the occasion? What special problems, if any, did you discover in the context, audience demographics, or audience dynamics?

## AUDIENCE ANALYSIS RESEARCH: CLASS PROFILE

**Purpose:** To provide practical experience in making inferences based on observation of an audience.

**Procedures:**

1. Use this exercise as an individual homework assignment. Ask students to do the following: Based on your observations of the class, complete an Audience Analysis Worksheet, using the class as the audience. In making topic-related comments, assume you will be speaking on "Raising Taxes for Educational Funding."

2. On the same day that you assign this exercise, take ten minutes to have the class complete the Attitude Survey on pages 74–75 of this *Guide*.

3. Tabulate the results of the Attitude Survey before the next class.

4. Discuss the Audience Analysis homework assignment, using the following questions:
• What kinds of demographic information did you list?
• On what grounds did you determine demographic information?
• What kinds of occasion factors did you list?
• How will you work to overcome problems caused by the context?
• What kinds of audience dynamics factors did you list?
• On what grounds did you infer the audience dynamics factors?

5. Distribute the tabulated responses to the Attitude Survey and discuss:
• Are there any results that surprise you? If so, what assumptions were you making incorrectly about the audience?

• In preparing for a speech, how important is accurate information about the audience?

• How can the results of this survey help you to prepare future speeches for this audience?

# ATTITUDE SURVEY

|  | Strongly Agree | | | | Strongly Disagree |
|---|---|---|---|---|---|
| 1. Higher education in the state needs more money. | 1 | 2 | 3 | 4 | 5 |
| 2. Public education in the state needs more money. | 1 | 2 | 3 | 4 | 5 |
| 3. College teachers deserve a pay raise. | 1 | 2 | 3 | 4 | 5 |
| 4. Public school teachers deserve a pay raise. | 1 | 2 | 3 | 4 | 5 |
| 5. I would be willing to pay more taxes in order to give college teachers a pay raise. | 1 | 2 | 3 | 4 | 5 |
| 6. I would be willing to pay more taxes in order to give public school teachers a pay raise. | 1 | 2 | 3 | 4 | 5 |
| 7. I would be willing to pay more taxes in order to increase the funding for higher education. | 1 | 2 | 3 | 4 | 5 |
| 8. I would be willing to pay more taxes in order to increase the funding for public education. | 1 | 2 | 3 | 4 | 5 |
| 9. Colleges and universities would have enough money if they cut the waste out of the system. | 1 | 2 | 3 | 4 | 5 |
| 10. Public education would have enough money if it cut the waste out of the system. | 1 | 2 | 3 | 4 | 5 |

11. I am: female _____ male _____

12. My age is: 17-22 _____; 23-30 _____; 31-40 _____; 41-50 _____; 51 or over _____.

13. My marital status is: married _____; single _____; widowed _____; divorced _____

14. My religion is: _____

15. My race is: white _____; black _____; Asian _____; Hispanic _____; other _____

16. My year in college is: 1st _____; 2nd _____; 3rd _____; 4th _____

17. My college major is: _____

18. My home state/country is: _____

19. I have _____ do not have _____ children.

20. The groups I belong to are: _____

## AUDIENCE ANALYSIS WORKSHEET

Audience: _____
Topic: _____

**Occasion/Context Factors**
Time _____          Date (day of week, other) _____
Location _____
Physical setting _____
Size of audience _____
Audience seating arrangement _____
Preliminary tuning _____
Recent events significant to group _____
Recent events significant to topic _____
Purpose of meeting _____

**Demographics**
Age _____          Sex _____
Educational level _____
Group affiliations _____
Sociocultural background _____

**Audience Dynamics**

Prior knowledge of topic _____

Prior knowledge of speaker _____

Probable needs _____

Probable attitudes/values _____

Attitude toward event _____

## "WHY SHOULD I CARE?"—A MOTIVATIONAL APPEAL EXERCISE

**Purpose:** To provide practice in discovering the needs of an audience.

**Procedures:** For each of the following topics, instruct students to list reasons why the audience should care about the topic and the "needs" being appealed to.

**Example:**
    Topic: Adding Insulation to Your Home
    Audience: home owners

| **Why audience should care:** | **Needs appealed to:** |
| --- | --- |
| Save money on heating bills | Economic security of family |
| Warmer home environment | Personal comfort—physiological need |
| Save environment by helping conserve fuel | Self-esteem and belonging to conservation movement |

**Topics/Audiences:**

1. Topic: How to Take a Painless Backpacking Trip

    Audience: beginning backpackers

2. Topic: Getting Better Grades by "Listening"

    Audience: college students

3. Topic: Spending a Semester at a University Overseas

    Audience: college students

4. Topic: Putting More Peak Experiences in Your Life

    Audience: general

5. Topic: Developing Your Personal Power

    Audience: general

6. Topic: Five Steps to a Safer Home

    Audience: general

7. Topic: How to Win the Dating Game

    Audience: college students

**Possible Answers:**

| **1. Why audience should care:** | **Needs appealed to:** |
| --- | --- |
| Avoid injuries | Safety |

Something to do with others        Belongingness
Get into better physical shape     Physiological

**2. Why audience should care:      Needs appealed to:**

Succeeding in college              Esteem / Security
Living up to potential             Self-actualization
Winning at the grading game        Dominance

**3. Why audience should care:      Needs appealed to:**

Join an elite group of students    Esteem / Belongingness
Develop broad perspective          Self-actualization
Get away from home/campus          Change
Get away from home restrictions    Independence

**4. Why audience should care:      Needs appealed to:**

Get the most out of life           Self-actualization
Belong to an elite group of people Belongingness / Esteem

**5. Why audience should care:      Needs appealed to:**

Being an asset at work             Security
Expanding your competence          Esteem
Winning over others                Dominance

**6. Why audience should care:      Needs appealed to:**

Fear of robbery                    Safety/security
Fear of personal injury            Safety/security

**7. Why audience should care:      Needs appealed to:**

Win respect of friends             Esteem
Satisfy biological urges           Physiological
Be in the elite group              Belongingness
Fear of diseases                   Safety
Have influence over others         Dominance

## WHAT'S THE NEED?

**Purpose:** To identify the motivational factors in advertisements.

**Procedures:**

1. Ask students to complete the following assignment: Bring a magazine or newspaper advertisement to the next class. If you do not have your own copy of a magazine or newspaper, photocopy an advertisement from a magazine in the library. Do not rip a page out of a library magazine!

2. Before the next class, prepare a deck of 3-by-5-inch index cards with one <u>need</u> written on each card. Prepare as many cards as you have students in the class. The needs listed in the text are: physiological, safety/security, belongingness, esteem, self-actualization, need for change, need for independence, and need for dominance.

If you wish to expand the need list, use a list like the eight needs commonly found in advertisements, from Vance Packard's *The Hidden Persuaders:*
   • Need for emotional security
   • Need to be reassured of one's personal worth
   • Need for ego gratification
   • Need for creative outlets
   • Need for love objects
   • Need for a sense of power
   • Need for roots (a sense of heritage)
   • Need for immortality

See also Charles U. Larson's adaptation of the Packard list in *Persuasion: Reception and Responsibility,* 3rd ed. (Belmont, Calif: Wadsworth Publishing Co., 1983), pp. 80–83.

3. As students enter the room the day of the exercise, instruct them to tape their advertisements on the walls of the room. Try to space them so all are visible. If you have a large classroom, you may wish to have half of the advertisements put on the front wall and half on the back wall. If you can, number the advertisements.

4. Then have each student draw a card from the deck of *Needs*. After drawing, give each student ten minutes to walk around the room and find two or three advertisements that appeal to the need drawn. After locating the advertisements, the students should write down their numbers or identifying names and note how the need is being appealed to in each advertisement.

5. Student reports: Starting at one side of the room, have each student in turn stand by one of his or her chosen advertisements and (a) briefly describe it for the class if it is too small for all to see, (b) state the *need* drawn, and (c) explain how the advertisement illustrates the need. If someone else has already used the same advertisement to explain the same need, the student should use his or her second or third choice.

## ADDITIONAL RESOURCES

Beatty, Michael J., and Stephen K. Payne, "Receiver Apprehension and Cognitive Complexity." *The Western Journal of Speech Communication* 45 (Fall 1981): 363–369.

Clevenger, Theodore. *Audience Analysis.* (Indianapolis: Bobbs-Merrill Co., Inc., 1966). This is a good but old source.

Franco, J. J. "Speaker, Know Thy Audience." *Training Development Journal* 39 (June 1985): 20–21.

Halloway, Hal. "An Exercise in Audience Analysis." *Communication Education* 33 (October 1984): 392–397.

Holtzman, Paula. *The Psychology of the Speaker's Audience.* (Glenview, Ill.: Scott, Foresman and Co., 1970).

Larson, Charles U. *Persuasion: Reception and Responsibility*, 3rd ed. (Belmont, Calif.: Wadsworth Publishing Co., 1983), Chap. 4.

"The Topic and the Audience." Films for the Humanities, 1982. Color, 15 minutes.

# 6

## Structuring Your Speech

### CHAPTER OBJECTIVES

After reading Chapter 6, students should be able to:

1. Name and apply the three principles of good form.

2. Identify ways to achieve greater simplicity and symmetry in a speech.

3. Create a research overview to help determine the main points of a speech.

4. Define and use the principles of good form to arrange main points.

5. Apply the rules for selecting supporting materials.

6. Explain and use the ideal model for the support of a main point.

7. Identify the functions of introductions and the introductory techniques.

8. Identify the functions of a conclusion and the techniques to develop an effective conclusion.

9. Define and use effective transitions, previews, and internal summaries in a speech.

# DISCUSSION (TEXT P. 171)

**1.** In discussion groups of five students, share your research overviews for your next speeches. What main points are suggested by each overview? What do you learn about the selection of main points from these discussions?

**Comments:** To help use this exercise, assign a research overview for the next speech. On the day the research overview is due, conduct this exercise in groups. You may want to assign the question "What main points are suggested by each overview?" Discussion of what was learned about selection of main points could include:

(a) Main points are often suggested by the way the material breaks down topically, categorically, and so on.

(b) The principles of good form should enter into the selection of main points.

(c) There are a variety of ways to organize a given topic. The selection of a way often depends on the audience analysis.

**2.** Share the structural plan of your next speech with a classroom partner, so that you become consultants for each other. Help each other come up with alternative patterns for the main points, introductions, and conclusions. After the speeches are presented, each consulting team should explain the options they considered and why they chose the particular structures used for each speech.

**Comments:** This exercise has two parts: a pre-speech consultation and a post-speech discussion. The pre-speech consultation is an excellent way to focus attention on the principles in the chapter and force students to spend time analyzing their choices. The post-speech discussion, which can be a written assignment if class discussion would take too much time, allows students to reflect on the need to consider options.

# APPLICATION (TEXT PP. 171–172)

**1.** Select a speech from Appendix B of this book and study its symmetry. Are its major parts—introduction, main points, and conclusion—coherent and properly balanced?

**Comments:** Following are some suggested responses to one of the speeches: "The Right Fuel," by Thressia Taylor is a good example for study because the speech is somewhat out of balance. Her introduction is appealing and effective. Her main points are clearly delineated and the conclusion is appropriate. This is a good speech, but it would have been better if each of the main points (needed nutrients) had been more fully developed. As presented, the introduction is almost as long as the body of the speech.

**2.** Analyze your favorite television advertisement in terms of structure. How does it arouse attention and gain credibility? What pattern of development does it use? Does the conclusion tie into the introduction? Present your analysis in class.

**Comments:** You could instruct students to describe their favorite advertisement in detail for members of the class who may not have seen it. (A surprising number of college students today seem not to watch television at all. If this seems to be the case with your class, expand the assignment to include radio advertisements.)

Comments on how an advertisement arouses attention might relate to attention-getting techniques: rhetorical question, quotation, story, involving the audience, relating the subject to personal experience, or startling the audience. Techniques other than the ones discussed in the chapter will emerge. Some examples are color, music, and action. Discussion should cover how different forms of communication can use both the abovementioned attention-getting devices and also make use of the unique features of the medium.

When analyzing how the advertisement gains credibility, you could center the discussion on the concept of identification. You may also wish to discuss how television often uses pseudocredibility—an actor who plays a doctor in a series or an actor who is dressed like a doctor assumes the credibility of a real doctor, for example.

The pattern of development employed by the advertisement could be selected from those discussed in the chapter (spatial, categorical, cause-effect, problem-solution, sequential) or be specifically described if it is a new pattern. Discussion can include how this particular pattern helps keep attention and interest or helps the message flow.

Conclusion-introduction links should be identified. Discussion should include whether or not this technique provides closure and is memorable.

**3.** What kind of supporting material would you use for each of the following thematic statements?

a. The Strategic Defense Initiative is an expensive fantasy that threatens world peace.

b. The *Challenger* space disaster could have been avoided with just a few structural changes.

c. It is better to live together than to marry.

d. We are destroying our own atmosphere.

e. Cambodia is the great untold tragedy of our time.

**Comments:** All answers should represent the ideal model for the support of a main point ("hard" information, the most authoritative judgment, a graphic story or example) and be congruent with the five rules for using supporting material to establish a point.

(a) SDI is controversial (rule 1), complex (rule 2), risky (rule 3), and far from a student's credibility area (rule 4). A combination of proofs is required—numerous types of hard data paired with examples to make them clearer, expert opinion, and thorough documentation of sources.

(b) The issue is complex (rule 2) and outside a student's credibility area (rule 4). Hard data, expert opinion, and examples or visual aids are all required to clarify the complex issues relating to this disaster.

(c) The topic is controversial (rule 1) and risky (rule 3). Hard data and lay testimony are recommended.

(d) The topic is complex (rule 2), outside a student's credibility area (rule 4), and far from personal life (rule 5). Hard data, expert opinion, thorough documentation, and vivid examples are recommended.

(e) The topic is controversial (rule 1), complex (rule 2), probably outside the student's area of expertise (rule 4), and far from the audience's personal life (rule 5). A combination of hard data, thorough documentation of sources, and vivid examples are recommended.

**4.** Frame a story you might tell in developing one of the thematic statements from Question 3. In groups of five, discuss how these stories might advance the purpose of the speech. Each group should nominate one story as the best in its group and present it to the class as a whole.

**Comments:** A variety of stories will be generated. If the stories are intended for the introduction, they should be brief. Discuss in class: Are the stories appropriate for this audience? Do they create audience identification with the speaker or topic? Would it be easy to create a link from this story to your thematic statement?

**5.** Suggest an appropriate structural pattern for each of the following speech purposes.

a. To inform listeners about where they might see a grizzly bear in wild America this summer.

b. To inform an audience about sexist advertising practices.

c. To inform an audience about the ideal way to prepare for an examination.

d. To persuade listeners to vote in the next election.

e. To persuade listeners to vote Republican (or Democratic) in the next election.

**Comments:** Several patterns are possible for each topic. If students offer problem-solution or cause-effect for informative purposes, remind them that it is very difficult to avoid persuading using those patterns.

(a) spatial
(b) categorical, perhaps sequential

(c) categorical or sequential

(d) problem-solution, cause-effect

(e) problem-solution, cause-effect

**6.** What kind of attention-getting introduction would you design for each of the topics listed in Question 5? What other specific techniques might be useful to introduce and conclude such speeches?

**Comments:**  Any answer using the introductory techniques discussed in the chapter may be appropriate. Watch for answers that begin with the thematic statement; these answers are incorrect, as the introductory functions of gaining attention are not met.

# ADDITIONAL EXERCISES*

## INTRODUCTORY TECHNIQUES

**Purpose:**  To compare and contrast introductory techniques.

**Procedures:**

1. Divide the class into work groups and assign to each group one of the speeches below.

   **a.** Informative speech: how to make purchases at auctions

   **b.** Persuasive speech: use your seat belts

   **c.** Informative speech: the safety measures in donating blood

   **d.** Persuasive speech: we need the Strategic Defense Initiative

   **e.** Informative speech: the academic advising procedures on campus

   **f.** Speech of celebration: Martin Luther King's Birthday

2. Instruct each group to create speech introductions using each of the introductory techniques appropriate for their topic. They should also add suitable remarks to enhance their credibility on the topic.

3. Have each group select the best introduction to present to the class.

---

*  If the class as a whole delivers poor introductions or conclusions after the applicable exercises in this section have been conducted, additional discussion will be necessary to correct the problem. One of the best ways to show a class a poor introductory technique is to edit all of the introductions from a set of speeches, put them on a videotape, and run the tape for the class, asking: "Would you be interested in hearing these speeches?" Editing a set of conclusions onto a separate videotape can illustrate a lack of summary, closure, and finality.

4. In class, discuss what criteria the groups used to select the best technique for the introduction.

## TRANSITIONS

**Purpose:** To identify transitions in speeches.

**Procedures:**

1. Select one of the speeches from Appendix B of the text.

2. Ask students to read this speech and to locate all the transitions, previews, and internal summaries in it. Also instruct students to locate places where additional transitions, previews, or internal summaries would help the flow of the speech.

3. In class, go through the speech, identifying the transitions, previews, and internal summaries. Next, ask if students located places where previews, internal summaries, or transitions would help the flow of the speech. Ask the students to phrase the transitions.

4. In class, discuss the importance of transitions to the orderly flow of the speech.

## INTRODUCTION ANALYSIS

**Purpose:** To categorize and evaluate introductory techniques.

**Procedures:**

1. This exercise can serve as an individual homework assignment or as a group assignment in class. Duplicate the sample introductions from Appendix A of this *Guide*.

2. For each sample introduction, instruct students to answer the following questions:

   **a.** Which introductory technique is used?

   **b.** Does the introduction fulfill its function?

   **c.** Is this a good, fair, or poor introduction?

   **d.** If it is fair or poor, how would you improve it?

3. Discuss in class: What separates a good introduction from the rest? How can you tell if your introduction is good when you are constructing a speech?

## CONCLUSION ANALYSIS

**Purpose:** To categorize and evaluate concluding techniques.

**Procedures:**

1. This exercise can be used as an individual homework assignment or as a group assignment in class. Duplicate the sample conclusions from Appendix B of this *Guide*.

2. For each conclusion, instruct students to answer the following questions:

   **a.** What concluding technique is used?

   **b.** Does the conclusion fulfill its function?

   **c.** Is this a good, fair, or poor conclusion?

   **d.** If it is fair or poor, how would you improve it?

3. Discuss in class: What separates a good conclusion from the rest? How can you tell if your conclusion is good when you are constructing a speech?

## ADDITIONAL RESOURCES

Daniels, Tom D., and Richard F. Whitman. "The Effects of Message Introduction, Message Structure, and Verbal Organizing Ability upon Learning of Message Information." *Human Communication Research* 7 (1981): 147–160.

Schiff, Roselyn L., et al. *Communication Strategy: A Guide to Speech Preparation.* (Glenview, Ill.: Scott, Foresman and Co., 1981).

"Basic Patterns of Organization." University of Iowa, 1959. 30 minutes.

# 7

## Outlining Your Speech

## CHAPTER OBJECTIVES

After reading Chapter 7, students should be able to:

1. Identify, develop, and use three types of outlines in preparing a speech.

2. Define and recognize the main points, subpoints, and sub-subpoints of an outline.

3. Name and apply the rules for formal outlining.

4. Properly word the main points of an outline.

5. Name three types of supporting materials and recognize where in an outline they usually appear.

6. Prepare proper reference citations.

# DISCUSSION (TEXT P. 196)

**1.** Working in groups of five students, present to your group a preparation outline of the next speech you plan to give in class. Explain the strategy of the structure and show how the outline satisfies the principles of coordination and subordination. Revise as appropriate in light of the group discussion that follows:

**Comments:** If time permits, this is an excellent question to force analysis of the outline and its content. You may also have students look for inadequacies or weaknesses in the introduction, preview, transitions, internal summaries, conclusion, or supporting materials. To facilitate the discussion, you might require students to bring five copies of their outline to class to share with members of their group.

**2.** Select one of the speeches from Appendix B of this book and prepare a formal outline of the speech. Does this outline help you understand the structure and strategy of the speech? Does the outline reveal any structural flaws? Can you see any different ways the speaker might have developed the speech? Present your thoughts on these questions in class discussion.

**Comments:** Outlines of two of these speeches can be found in Appendix C of this *Guide*.

**3.** If a successful speech is a bridge of meaning that joins speaker and listeners, then how would you describe the importance of an outline for the speech? Can you think of other metaphors that might describe the significance of outlines in public speaking?

**Comments:** This question utilizes metaphor as a means of describing the usefulness of outlining. The emphasis, however, should not be the metaphor, but rather the necessity and usefulness of outlines as a part of the speech preparation process. (Outlining is the glue that helps the speech stick together; an outline is a skeleton, not visible to the eye but necessary to hold the structure upright.)

# APPLICATION (TEXT PP. 196–197)

**1.** Assume that the speeches you give in class this semester will be advertised in advance in the campus newspaper. Develop titles that might be useful in attracting an audience to these speeches.

**Comments:** Have students create titles for their next speeches and post the titles instead of the names of the speakers for that set of speeches. After the speeches, discuss: Did the titles create anticipation for any of the speeches? What about the titles created the anticipation? Did speakers deliver on what was promised in the titles? When the speech and title differ, how do you feel as an audience member?

**2.** See if you can "unjumble" the following outline of the body of a speech, using the principles of coordination and subordination correctly.

Thematic statement: Deer hunting with a camera can be an exciting sport.

I. There is a profound quiet, a sense of mystery.

    A. The woods in late fall are enchanting.
        1. The "film-hunter" becomes part of a beautiful scene.
        2. Dawn is especially lovely.

    B. Example of big doe walking under my tree stand.
        1. When they appear, deer always surprise you.
        2. Example of big buck after long stalk.

II. Hunting from a stand can be a good way to capture a deer on film.

    A. The stalk method is another way to hunt with a camera.
        1. Learn to recognize deer tracks and droppings.
           a. Learn to recognize deer signs.
           b. Learn to recognize rubs on trees and scrapes on the ground.
        2. Hunt with the wind and move slowly.

    B. There are two main ways to hunt with a camera.
        1. Stands offer elevation above the line of sight and line of scent.
        2. Portable stands are also available.
        3. Locating and building your permanent stand.

III. The right camera can be no more expensive than a rifle.

    A. Selecting the right camera for film-hunting is essential.

    B. Certain features—like a "zoom" lens—are required.

IV. Display slide of Doe.

    A. You can collect "trophies" you can enjoy forever.

    B. Display slide of Buck.

    C. Not all hunters are killers: the film-hunter celebrates life, not death.

**Comments:** Answers may vary somewhat. The following rearrangement is recommended:

I. The "film-hunter" becomes part of a beautiful scene.

    A. The woods in late fall are enchanting.
        1. There is a profound quiet, a sense of mystery.
        2. Dawn is especially lovely.

    B. When they appear, deer always surprise you.
        1. Example of big doe walking under my tree stand.
        2. Example of big buck after long stalk.

II. There are two main ways to hunt with a camera.

    A. Hunting from a stand can be a good way to capture a deer on film.
        1. Stands offer elevation above the line of sight and line of scent.
        2. Locating and building your permanent stand.
        3. Portable stands are also available.

    B. The stalk method is another way to hunt with a camera.
        1. Hunt with the wind and move slowly.
        2. Learn to recognize deer signs.
            a. Learn to recognize tracks and droppings.
            b. Learn to recognize rubs on trees and scrapes on the ground.

III. Selecting the right camera for film-hunting is essential.

    A. Certain features—like "zoom" lens—are required.

    B. The right camera can be no more expensive than a rifle.

IV. You can collect "trophies" you can enjoy forever.

    A. Display slide of the Doe.

    B. Display slide of the Buck.

    C. Not all hunters are killers: the film-hunter celebrates life, not death.

# ADDITIONAL EXERCISES

## OUTLINE SCRAMBLE

**Purpose:** To analyze the logic of a detailed outline

**Procedures:**

    1. Duplicate the Outline Scramble on pages 94–95 of this *Guide*.

2. Ask students to unscramble the outline. Tell them to insert in the appropriate places the words *Introduction*, *Body*, and *Conclusion*.

3. Discuss in class the clues students used to deduce the outline (previews, parallelism, summary). The Unscrambled Outline appears on pages 96–97 of this *Guide*.

## ADDITIONAL RESOURCES

Hufman, Melody. "The Maze as an Instructional Instrument for Public Speaking." *Communication Education* 34 (January 1985): 63–68.

Schiff, Roselyn L., et al. *Communication Strategy: A Guide to Speech Preparation.* (Glenview, Ill.: Scott, Foresman and Co., 1981).

"The Outline." Films for the Humanities. 15 minutes.

## OUTLINE SCRAMBLE: MAKING A BID TO SAVE MONEY AT AUCTIONS

**Specific Purpose:**  To inform the audience how to make purchases at auctions

1. The right auction for you is easy to find.

2. Rule of auctions: Merchandise goes to the highest bidder.

3. Bid up to your limit, then stop.

4. Story of wagon wheel purchase and describe how they look in my garden.

5. "Choice" item.

6. Determine if the merchandise is in good shape and is what you really want.

7. Today we've learned how auctions work, how to find them, and how to make wise purchases at them.

8. "Times the money."

9. Fit the type of auction to your personal needs by following two steps: making a wish list and reading the auction listings.

10. Farm auction.

11. Example: my wish list contained wagon wheels and canning jars.

12. Now you are ready to go to the auction and learn how to make wise purchases using these four tips.

13. "Roundup."

14. After inspecting, be alert to when your item goes up for sale.

15. Pay attention to the "terms of the sale."

16. Estate auction.

17. Describe types of auctions.

18. Story of pricing wagon wheels at antique stores, being shocked, and deciding to find another way to make the purchase.

19. Today, let's look at how auctions work, where to find them, and tips on making purchases at auctions.

20. Auctions operate like any business.

21. Show auction section in the local Sunday newspaper as the way to find the auction.

22. Auctions are the other way to make purchases.

23. Quote National Association of Auctioneers' definition of auctions.

24. Thematic statement: Auctions are a way to have fun while saving money on the goods we need.

25. Other kinds of auctions that aren't for the average person.

26. Show an auction listing for an estate sale with jars and wagon wheels.

27. Arrive early to inspect the merchandise you're interested in.

28. Set a maximum amount on what you are willing to pay for this specific merchandise, considering its condition.

# UNSCRAMBLED OUTLINE: MAKING A BID TO SAVE MONEY AT AUCTIONS

**Specific Purpose:**  To inform the audience how to make purchases at auctions.

**Thematic Statement:**  Auctions are a way to have fun while saving money on the goods we need.

I. Introduction

    A. Story of pricing wagon wheels at antique stores, being shocked, and deciding to find another way to make the purchase.

    B. Auctions are the other way to make purchases.

    C. Today, let's look at how auctions work, where to find them, and tips on making purchases at auctions.

II. Body

    A. Auctions operate like any business.
        1. Quote National Association of Auctioneers' definition of auctions.
        2. Rule of auctions: merchandise goes to the highest bidder.

    B. The right auction for you is easy to find.
        1. Show auction section in the local Sunday newspaper as the way to find the auction.
        2. Describe types of auctions.
            a. Estate auction.
            b. Farm auction.
            c. Other kinds of auctions that aren't for the average person.
        3. Fit the type of auction to your personal needs by following two steps: making a wish list and reading the auction listings.
            a. Example: My wish list contained wagon wheels and canning jars.
            b. Show an auction listing for an estate sale with jars and wagon wheels.

    C. Now you are ready to go to the auction and learn how to make wise purchases using these four tips.
        1. Arrive early to inspect the merchandise you're interested in.
            a. Determine if the merchandise is in good shape and is what you really want.
            b. Set a maximum amount on what you are willing to pay for this specific merchandise, considering its condition.
        2. After inspecting, be alert to when your item goes up for sale.

3. Pay attention to the "terms of the sale."
   a. "Choice" item.
   b. "Times the money."
   c. "Roundup."
4. Bid up to your limit, then stop.

III. Conclusion

A. Today we've learned how auctions work, how to find them, and how to make wise purchases at them.

B. Story of wagon wheel purchase and describe how they look in my garden.

# 8

## Visual Aids

## CHAPTER OBJECTIVES

After reading Chapter 8, students should be able to:

1. Understand the major advantages visual aids bring to a speech.

2. Identify the different kinds of visual aids and list the advantages and disadvantages of each.

3. Describe three types of graphs and four types of charts, and explain how each can best serve a speech.

4. Identify the materials used for visual aids and list the advantages and disadvantages of each.

5. State four principles for designing visual aids.

6. State some basic guidelines for planning, practicing, and presenting visual aids.

# DISCUSSION (TEXT PP. 225–226)

**1.** Watch the national news programs on television and observe how graphics and pictures are used in combination with words to convey meaning clearly and effectively. What techniques are useful? Be prepared to discuss examples of effective and ineffective usage in class.

**Comments:** To find more examples of ineffective usage, you may wish to expand the assignment to include local as well as national news. Generally, newscasts use videotapes, graphic inserts of words or symbols (that represent fire, wreck, and so on), and maps. Ineffective usage is often technical (wrong film, wrong graphic, no graphic) but can also be poor choice of graphics (for example, discussing a minor wreck while showing the shot of an injured person sends a mixed message).

Note that the media's use of visual aids often is to maintain attention and to supplement the message. Research into what constitutes news suggests that many stations do not consider items as stories unless they have some graphic or visual dimension. In class, discuss if this practice is good or bad for newscasting.

**2.** Recall classes in which your instructors used visual aids. Did these aids serve one or more of the four functions of visual aids (aid understanding, authenticate or prove the point, add variety, or give lasting impact to the message)? Why or why not?

**Comments:** Experiences will vary widely. Common bad experiences include: instructors writing so much on the board that students see only their backs, instructors drawing illegible figures on the board, overhead projections being too small, equipment not working, instructors hunting around on a videotape for the clip to be shown. Typical good experiences include: well-planned, well-run videotapes and movies; overhead projections that effectively explain concepts; neat, legible writing or drawing on the blackboard; successful use of models to explain processes; and costuming to add interest to a subject.

In class, try to determine what made the usage effective or ineffective. Also discuss how much planning and practice is required to use visual aids properly.

**3.** Describe situations in which speakers either would or would not be effective visual aids for their own speeches. Have you ever seen examples outside your classroom in which speakers as visual aids worked against their own speeches?

**Comments:** Generally, the speaker is *not* a good visual aid when the topic and speaker together present some mixed message—for example, overweight individuals demonstrating the advantages of exercise or weak individuals demonstrating weightlifting. When speakers demonstrate situations outside their sphere of competence, they not only give a mixed message to the audience but may also embarrass themselves. Speakers are good visual aids when they appear to fit the subject and are competent (an athletic person demonstrating athletic feats).

**4.** Look through a recent popular magazine and analyze the advertisements according to the principles of design discussed here. Do the visual aspects of the ads work in concert with the words to emphasize the message? Which of the ads seem most balanced and pleasing to the eye? Do any of the ads violate the rules of simplicity and ease of comprehension? Which of the ads use color most and least effectively? Bring the most interesting ads to class and discuss your findings.

**Comments:** Librarians appreciate your reminding students not to rip advertisements out of library magazines. Generally, advertisements are good subjects for evaluating the general principles of balance, simplicity, and the like. Remind students, however, that advertisements contain much more detail than the visual aids used in speeches and should not be used as models for content.

Some teachers collect discarded visual aids and bring them to class as examples of effective or ineffective design principles.

## APPLICATION (TEXT P. 226)

**1.** Select a speech in Appendix B and prepare the rough draft of a visual aid that might have been used with it. Would the aid have helped when presenting the speech?

**Comments:** This exercise can serve as a group assignment, using the same speech or separate speeches for each group. Divide the class into groups and assign a different speech to each group, or divide the class into groups after everyone has read the same speech as homework.

You may also wish to ask students to specify when they would reveal the visual aid and if they would conceal it after use.

"Women in Politics: Time for a Change" could use a line chart showing jobless rates or increases in the number of poor (although aids of this type are not traditionally used in this speaking situation).

"The Right Fuel" could use drawings of a person with a plate hung under his or her nose saying "Feed this body nourishing food only" (although it is not necessary to convey the idea). The speech could also use a pie chart showing the proportions of protein, carbohydrates, fat, vitamins, minerals, and water needed.

"Are the Skies That Friendly?" could use a pie chart showing the percentage of qualified air controllers or a map of airport density in the Los Angeles area.

2.  What kinds of visual aids might be useful for the following speech topics?

a. Nuclear waste disposal sites in the United States

b. What to do in case of snake bite

c. History of the stock market over the last decade

d. How the federal budget is divided into major categories

e. Development of weapons systems in Russia and America

f. Administering your university: who has the power to do what?

g. How we got the modern telephone: the growth of an invention

h. Hunger in Africa: the human story

i. The sounds of navigation and what they mean

**Comments:**  Answers will vary somewhat.

(a) Map showing waste disposal sites
(b) Snake bite kit; poster with sequence of things to do
(c) Line graph showing growth over time
(d) Pie graph
(e) Bar graph comparing weapons; pictographs
(f) Flow chart
(g) Sequence chart showing stages of the invention
(h) Pie graphs showing proportion of hungry; bar graph showing trend of change in number of hungry; and so on
(i) Audiotape

# ADDITIONAL EXERCISES

## VISUAL AID ADAPTATION

**Purpose:**  To find solutions to common problems with visual aids

**Procedures:**

1. Use this exercise as an individual homework assignment or as a group task during class. Ask students to relate how they would solve the problems listed below, under Step 2.

2. Have each group or student present one problem and solution. Then discuss: Is this the best way to solve the problem? Are there other solutions? Does the solution have problems of its own?

**a.** You have found the perfect photograph to illustrate the concept, but it is very small.

**b.** You have found a commercially prepared map of the area you wish to discuss.

**c.** Your speech on the *Titanic* needs a visual aid showing where the iceberg breached the ship. You have found a suitable drawing in a book.

**d.** You are the second speaker, and the first speaker had already drawn his visual aids on the chalkboard when you arrived in class.

**e.** The previous speaker leaves his visual aids drawn on the chalkboard.

**f.** You are speaking on the second day. On the first day, all the speakers who had set their poster boards on the chalk tray had trouble. The boards kept falling on the floor during the speeches.

**g.** You have several small visual aids to be used in the middle of your speech. They need to be set out in advance so you can reach each one quickly when you get to the appropriate point in the speech.

**Answers will vary.**

(a) Have the photograph enlarged into a poster, or (if the detail is not important) use an overhead projector to cast a larger image that you can trace onto a poster board. If enlargement strategies don't work, offer the photograph only after your speech is finished.

(b) Trace the amount of detail you need onto a poster board. Do not use a map with too much detail.

(c) Use an overhead projector to trace the drawing onto a poster board, or neatly sketch the adaptation you need to illustrate your speech. Enlarge the drawing on a photocopier.

(d) Trade speaker positions with the second speaker, or pull down a screen to cover the distractions.

(e) Erase them.

(f) Visual aids are notorious for falling off chalk trays because chalk trays were not made to hold visual aids. The trays also remove the speaker too far from the audience.

Ask the instructor for an easel, or borrow one from your educational media department. Place the easel where everyone can see your visual aid. If an easel is not available, use masking tape. Always remove the aid when you are finished.

(g) Set them on a tray covered with a towel or cloth. Put them in a box that you can reach into easily but that the audience can't see into. Be certain the box is neat. Stack them on a shelf under the lectern.

## VISUAL AID PRESENTATION OF STATISTICS

**Purpose:** To determine which type of chart or graph best presents various types of statistics

**Procedures:**

1. Divide the class into work groups, and assign each group one of the statistics listed below, under Step 2. Have each group select the best two methods of presenting the information.

2. Have each group report to the class. Then discuss: How did you decide which method of presentation was best? How hard or easy would it be to prepare visual aids of this type? How helpful would they be in facilitating the audience's understanding of the statistics?

All of the following statistics are taken from the *Uniform Crime Reports for the United States* (Washington, D.C.: Federal Bureau of Investigation, U.S. Department of Justice, 1985).

**a.** The percentage of annual total burglaries by month: Jan. 8.2%; Feb. 7.2%; Mar. 8.2%; Apr. 7.8%; May 8.0%; June 7.9%; July 9.0%; Aug. 9.1%; Sept. 8.5%; Oct. 9.0%; Nov. 8.5%; Dec. 8.8%.

**b.** Larceny analysis: 1% purse snatchings; 1% pocket pickings; 1% coin machine; 14% shoplifting; 8% bicycles; 20% motor vehicles; 17% motor vehicle accessories; 23% other.

**c.** Motor vehicle theft by region: Northeast: auto 89.8%; truck 5.2%; other 5%. Midwest: auto 79%; truck 10.2%; other 10.8%. Southwest: auto 69.1%; truck 18.9%; other 12%. Western: auto 66.2%; truck 20.3%; other 13.5%. Total motor vehicle theft: auto 75.4%; truck 14.2%; other 10.4%.

**d.** Crime by region: Northeast: 20.8% of total population; 16% murders. Midwest: 24.8% of population; 19.5% murders. Southwest: 34.3% of population; 43% murders. Western: 20% of population; 21.4% murders.

**e.** One violent crime is recorded every 24 seconds; one property crime every 3 seconds; one murder every 28 minutes; one forcible rape every 6 minutes; one robbery every 63 seconds; one aggravated assault every 44 seconds.

## SELECTION OF VISUAL AID

**Purpose:** To analyze which type of aid best illustrates a speech concept

**Procedures:**

1. Divide the class into groups. Assign to each group one of the speech concepts listed below, under Step 2.

2. Ask each group to decide which type of visual aid best illustrates its concept. Have each group report its answer to the class.

   a. Perils of the Oregon Trail

   b. How to shear sheep

   c. Differences between the sound of a record and a compact disc

   d. Massage

   e. The need to use sunscreen

   f. Kayaking

**Answers will vary widely.**

(a) Maps showing the trail, maps with symbols representing the perils, pie charts showing causes of death of pioneers on the trail

(b) Poster board sketch, videotape, slides (Using a real sheep or, as one of my students once did, using a classmate to pretend to be a sheep would be a distraction, not an aid.)

(c) A phonograph and compact disc player connected to the same stereo speakers, plus a record and compact disc of the same recording

(d) A trained model who will not upstage your speech by groaning or smiling blissfully

(e) Graphs or charts of skin-cancer incidence and growth

(f) Model, some equipment (but probably not the kayak)

# ADDITIONAL RESOURCES

Lamberski, R. J., and F. M. Dwyer. "Exploratory Studies in the Effectiveness of Visual Illustrations." *AV Communication Review* 18 (1970): 235–240.

LeRoux, Paul. "The Fine Art of Show and Tell." *Working Woman* 10 (September 1985): 126–130.

O'Malley, Christopher. "Making Quick Presentations: How to Get Better Visuals in Minutes." *Personal Computing* 9 (December 1985): 76–83.

Seiler, William J. "The Effects of Visual Materials on Attitudes, Credibility, and Retention." *Speech Monographs* 38 (November 1971): 331–334.

"Aids to Speaking." Centron film (videotape). Coronet/MTI Film & Video Co. 15 minutes.

"Choosing the Audio-Visual Dimension." Films for the Humanities. 15 minutes.

# 9

## The Speaker's Language

## CHAPTER OBJECTIVES

After reading Chapter 9, students should be able to:

1. Understand the five powers of language.

2. Describe the common barriers that language must overcome to awakening feelings.

3. Know what techniques can help listeners see, feel, get a sense of group identity, act, and remember.

4. Know the difference between archetypes and culturetypes.

5. Define rhetorical style.

6. Implement the five C's of language: clarity, color, concreteness, correctness, and conciseness.

# DISCUSSION (TEXT PP. 257–258)

**1.** The example that opens this chapter presents arguments for and against whiskey, using connotative language. Rephrase these arguments, using denotative language. How does this change affect the power of the arguments? What speech situations call for more denotative language? How can connotative language be misused? When is it most appropriate?

**Comments:** Rephrased quotation:

A legislator was asked how he felt about whiskey. He replied, "If, when you say alcohol, you mean that beverage that causes people to act irrationally and that disrupts family interactions because of the money that is spent on it, that makes people behave in less than desirable ways until they can no longer maintain a decent standard of living, then certainly I am against it with all my power.

But if, when you say alcohol, you are referring to social drinking that helps people relate better with one another, that is used on special, festive occasions, and which helps to build the state coffers through the taxes that are levied upon it, taxes used to provide social services and amenities for our citizens, then certainly I am in favor of it."

Rephrased, the arguments are less vivid and do not invite us to see the words emotionally. Situations where precise language is needed—for example, medical treatment or situations that are emotionally volatile—require denotative speech. Connotative language is often misused to short-circuit the reasoning process or to misdirect our attention. Connotative language is appropriate when it helps us to see or feel the impact of a situation.

**2.** In the 1950s, Richard Weaver suggested that *progress* was the prime culturetype of American society. What words do you nominate as culturetypes in contemporary society? Why? How are they used now in public communication? Share with the entire class examples from several speeches, essays, editorials, cartoons, or advertisements.

**Comments:** Culturetypes might include: The western frontier or the Horatio Alger myth. Student analysis of advertisements will uncover other possibilities. A symbol or image is a culturetype when its use is widespread and it symbolizes the way people in a given society view themselves.

**3.** How can specific language techniques be abused in public communication? Bring examples to class.

**Comments:** Abuse entails any use that distracts from clear understanding of the overall meaning or attempts to misdirect attention and reasoning for covert purposes. Advertisements are excellent places to find misuse of techniques, particularly hyperbole. Political advertisements are good places to find oversimplification.

**4.** Analyze how you used the power of language in your last speech. What if any barriers to perception or feeling did you have to overcome, and what techniques did you use? Could you have improved the effectiveness of your language? How?

**Comments:** Students will find their language use was not as powerful as it could have been. After identifying the barrier(s) inherent in their topics, have students change the language in one part of their speeches, using one of the suggested techniques for overcoming barriers. As a short speech assignment, have each student redo and present a one-minute segment of his or her speech where language techniques would help overcome the barriers of the topic.

# APPLICATION (TEXT P. 258)

**1.** Use archetypal metaphors to describe the following abstract concepts:

friendship                          brotherhood
freedom                             democracy
justice                             poverty

Present your descriptions in class. Which work most effectively and why?

**Comments:**  A variety of answers is possible:

*friendship:* a glow of light in a cold and dark world
*freedom:* the light of hope for the world
*justice:* a war against the dark side
*brotherhood:* strong walls of comfort against the storm
*democracy:* holistic medicine for an ailing world
*poverty:* a cancer spreading throughout the land

In class, have each student contribute his or her archetypal metaphor for the first concept. Instruct students to note the ones that are particularly effective. Discuss which metaphors are found effective by the class as a whole. Evaluate what these metaphors have that the others do not. Continue the procedure for the rest of the concepts.

**2.** Study the language customs and strategies in a speech from a political campaign. How is the power of language exercised? What special tools are used? Evaluate the effectiveness of this usage according to the standards discussed here.

**Comments:** This assignment could become time-intensive. A campaign must be located; speech or printed artifacts must be secured and analyzed. If a campaign is active on the campus, the application could be done as a group assignment: instruct students to secure one artifact from the campaign and analyze it for linguistic techniques. If the instructor has access to longer political advertisements from the last election, they might serve as a basis for analysis.

As an alternative assignment, have students analyze the language in a recent local or national advertising campaign (Pepsi, Coke, McDonald's, for example).

**3.** Determine from their published pamphlets and speeches the heroes and villains of the peace, anti-apartheid, gay liberation, and women's liberation movements.

**Comments:** These materials may not be readily available in the library. By contacting such groups ahead of time you can obtain materials for use in class. You may wish to concentrate on one of the areas, such as the peace movement. Students can find up-to-date information on the activities of such groups in *Facts on File*.

**4.** To explore and help develop stylistic techniques, your instructor will assign different language tools to members of the class and then present a subject. Your talk will be to make a statement about this subject using the technique you have been assigned. Share these statements in class. Try this exercise several times, using different subjects and different tools of language. Evaluate in class what this exercise reveals about the power, techniques, and standards of language.

This assignment could also be done by teams. Have each team write their linguistic technique on a tear sheet from a flip chart and tape it to the wall by their seats (to give visual emphasis to the device).

Stylistic devices include: simile, metaphor, simplification, synecdoche, metonymy, onomatopoeia, incongruity, hyperbole, personification, inclusive pronouns, culturetypes, archetypal metaphor, alliteration, anaphora, inversion, antithesis.

Subjects for this exercise could include:
• Why you should register for classes early
• What it's like to find parking on campus
• Cocaine
• Buying a computer
• Studying for tests

**5.** President Reagan is noted for his skillful use of culturetypes and rhetorical examples. Read his *"Challenger* Memorial Speech" in Appendix B and identify the language tools he relies on most heavily.

**Comments:** The major culturetype in Reagan's *"Challenger* Memorial Speech" is the frontier metaphor, extended to space exploration. For further development of this idea, see Janice Hacker Rushing, "Ronald Reagan's 'Star Wars' Address: Mythic Containment of Technical Reasoning," *Quarterly Journal of Speech* 72 (1986): 415–433. Discussion might focus on the concept of the frontier in American culture; see Frederick Jackson Turner, "The Significance of the Frontier in American History," in *The Turner Thesis* (Boston: Heath, 1956), pp. 1–18, and Ronald H. Carpenter, "Frederick Jackson Turner and the Rhetorical Impact of the Frontier Thesis," *Quarterly Journal of Speech* 63 (1977): 117–129.

You might also wish to ask students to identify the following techniques in Reagan's speech:

a. metaphor (frontier culturetype, family archetype)

b. archetypes (family, sons and daughters of our nation)

c. antithesis (when we reach for the stars, we fall short)

d. anaphora (We remember . . . We remember . . .)

e. rhetorical example (Dick Scobee example)

f. personification (stirred the soul of our nation)

# ADDITIONAL EXERICSES

## SIMILE AND METAPHOR PRACTICE

**Purpose:** To practice creating similes and metaphors to clarify abstract subjects

**Procedures:**

1. Use this exercise as an individual homework assignment or as a group assignment in class. Ask students to create both a simile and a metaphor to clarify what is meant by the following:

   a. Sister/brotherhood of Greek life on campus

   b. Satisfaction of climbing a mountain

   c. Poor posture

   d. Awkward silence

   e. Preventative medicine

2. Have each student or group share a simile or a metaphor of the first topic. Instruct students to jot down notes on their favorite similes/metaphors. After discussing the first subject, repeat the procedure for the remaining subjects.

3. Discuss: What similes/metaphors were the most effective? What sets them apart from the rest of the similes/metaphors? What cautions do you need to remember when using similes or metaphors in your speeches?

## PERSONIFICATION PRACTICE

**Purpose:** To practice creating personifications

**Procedures:**

1. Use this exercise as an individual homework assignment or as a group task in class. Ask students to create an example using personification for each of the following:

   **a.** The YWCA as an organization

   **b.** Our national forests

   **c.** A Las Vegas casino

   **d.** The local power company

2. Have each student or group share a personification of the first topic. Instruct students to jot down notes on their favorite personifications. After discussing the first subject, repeat the procedure for the remaining subjects.

3. Discuss: What techniques were the most effective? What sets them apart from the rest? What cautions do you need to remember when using these techniques in your speeches?

## TECHNIQUES TO CREATE GROUP IDENTITY

**Purpose:** To practice techniques for creating group identity

**Procedures:**

1. Use this exercise as an individual homework assignment. Ask students to create an introduction to a speech for each of the audiences below, using inclusive pronouns, references to common or group history, and/or god-terms for that group. (If it is helpful, you may select a topic for each audience.)

   **a.** Faculty senate

   **b.** Chamber of commerce

   **c.** Classmates in public speaking

   **d.** Residents of a dormitory

   **e.** Local P.T.A.

2. When making the assignment, offer an example such as: "As members of the university, we are all familiar with the traditional battles that are waged every year—inadequate salary increases, inadequate departmental budgets, and inadequate time."

## ANALYSIS OF LINGUISTIC TECHNIQUES IN A SPEECH

**Purpose:** To identify and analyze linguistic techniques in a speech

**Procedures:**

1. Locate a speech high in linguistic content and duplicate it for the class.

2. Ask students to read the speech and identify all of the linguistic techniques. If this exercise is used as a group assignment in class, assign one page to each of five groups.

3. Discuss in class the linguistic techniques discovered during students' analysis. Are there too many? How does the amount of substantive proof compare with the amount of linguistic techniques in this speech?

# ADDITIONAL RESOURCES

Bosmajiam, Haig A., ed. *Dissent: Symbolic Behavior and Rhetorical Strategies* (Boston: Allyn and Bacon, 1972).

Bowers, John Waite, and Donovan J. Ochs. *The Rhetoric of Agitation and Control* (Reading, Mass.: Addison-Wesley Publishing Co., 1971).

Campbell, Karlyn K. *The Rhetorical Act* (Belmont, Calif.: Wadsworth Publishing Co., 1982).

Chronkhite, Gary. "Perception and Meaning." In *Handbook of Rhetorical and Communication Theory*, Carroll C. Arnold and John Waite Bowers, ed. (Boston: Allyn and Bacon, 1984); figures of speech, pp. 183–185.

Edelman, Murray. *Political Language: Words That Succeed and Policies That Fail* (New York: Academic Press, 1977).

Salter, Marty M., Deborah Weider-Hatfield, and Donald L. Rubin. "Generic Pronoun Use and Perceived Speaker Credibility." *Communication Quarterly* 31 (Spring 1983): 180–184.

Scott, Robert L., and Wayne Brockriede. *The Rhetoric of Black Power* (New York: Harper & Row, 1969).

Siltanen, Susan A. "The Persuasiveness of Metaphor: A Replication and Extension." *The Southern Speech Communication Journal* 47 (Fall 1981): 67–83.

"Style in Language." Films for the Humanities. 15 minutes.

# 10

---

# Presenting Your Speech

## CHAPTER OBJECTIVES

After reading Chapter 10, students should be able to:

1. Distinguish between delivering and presenting a speech.

2. Identify, differentiate among, and list the strengths and weaknesses of each method of presentation.

3. Describe the relationship between vocal qualities and speaker ethos.

4. Determine their optimum pitch.

5. Determine if their habitual rate of speaking is within acceptable norms.

6. Achieve vocal variety for a more effective presentation.

7. Differentiate among articulation, pronunciation, and dialect.

8. Identify three dimensions of effective nonverbal communication.

9. Describe the ideal use of facial expression, eye contact, body movement, gestures, and personal appearance.

10. List and implement the steps of practicing a speech.

# DISCUSSION (TEXT P. 286)

**1.** Attend a public speaking event in your community, such as a lecture at your college, a political speech, or a church service. Did the speaker read from a manuscript, make a memorized presentation, or speak extemporaneously? Was the speaker's voice effective or ineffective? Why? How would you evaluate the speaker's use of body language? Discuss your observations with your classmates.

**Comments:** First, discuss the type of presentation (memorized, extemporaneous, and so on). How can you tell the difference between an extemporaneous and another presentation type? Did the type of presentation seem appropriate for the occasion? Would this speaker have been better served by a different type of presentation?

Second, discuss vocal effectiveness. Which dimensions of the speaker's voice were particularly effective or ineffective (pitch, rate, loudness, variety, articulation, pronunciation, dialect)? What specifically annoyed you or helped keep your attention? Did the vocal presentation affect your perception of ethos?

Finally, discuss body language. What elements of eye contact, facial expression, body movement, gesture, or dress were particularly effective or ineffective? Did any of these elements affect your perceptions of the speaker's credibility? If you could recommend one change to the speaker, what would it be?

**2.** Become an observer of nonverbal communication in social groups. Look at people's facial expressions, their gestures, their movements in communication. Discuss how these are similar or dissimilar to those used by effective speakers.

**Comments:** Discussion should focus on the following questions:

• Do good speakers use the same number and variety of facial expressions as people in conversations? Answer: The best speakers have very expressive faces and do not try to hide their feelings from the audience.

• How do speakers' gestures differ? Answer: Speakers should not use repetitive punctuation gestures (beat out the rhythm of the idea), body-touching movements, such as playing with hair or rubbing an arm. Speakers will use a variety of natural gestures as illustrators (show how big, how wide).

• How does the movement of good speakers differ from that of persons in conversation? Answer: This area may show the biggest difference, as speakers use movement strategically—to show movement within the speech structure (at a transition) or to emphasize an important point. Movement is saved for the moments that require emphasis or change. Movement in conversation is more random.

**3.** Discuss the impact that voice and appearance may have on an audience. Share with your classmates an example of an instance in which voice or appearance negatively affected a speaker's ethos.

**Comments:** Students will have a variety of answers, from overdressed to underdressed. If discussion is slow, you may wish to begin with the way professors dress and then expand to other arenas. Would some clothing practices be appropriate on campus and not appropriate elsewhere in the community? Are clothing norms the same in various regions of the country? (I went through a phase where I wore cowboy boots, even when consulting. In Idaho, this mode of dress was only slightly outside the norm of business dress. However, if I had been working in New York or in the Midwest, my clothing would have appeared more out of place.)

## APPLICATION (TEXT PP. 286–287)

**1.** Exchange your self-evaluation tape with a classmate and write a critique of the other speaker's voice and articulation. Make specific recommendations for improvement. Work on your classmate's recommendations for you in oral practice, then make a second tape to share with your partner. Do you see signs of improvement with each other's performance?

**Comments:** To implement this exercise, require students to make a self-evaluation tape, as described in the chapter, and to bring it to class the day you make this assignment. You may wish to caution students not to try to change their pitch in harmful ways. Discuss in class or require a written report on the degree of improvement resulting from this exercise.

**2.** Make a list of words you often mispronounce. Practice saying these words correctly for a week. See if you notice any carry-over of these changes into social conversation.

**Comments:** Students may wish to ask friends or family to help them determine a list of 10 words they often mispronounce. Require students to submit their list of words at the beginning of the week and a written, one-page response paper after the trial period.

**3.** Speculate on how you think people respond to your voice and appearance. Conduct a "reality check" by asking class members to discuss their actual perceptions of these qualities.

**Comments:** You may wish to structure this assignment by distributing a form like the Voice and Appearance Check List on page 119 of this *Guide*. Have students privately check the characteristics that apply to themselves. Then have students conduct the "reality check" in groups of three. Each of the three group members fills out the form on the other two members. Students can then exchange forms and discuss their perceptions.

**4.** Experiment with reading the same material aloud at different rates of speed and with varying loudness. Do these differences seem to affect the meaning of the material?

**Comments:** This exercise can be done with almost any material. The rate and loudness should affect the meanings. In class you could have students read the same short passage in accordance with your instructions: loud, soft, fast, slow. Discussion could center on how the meaning changed with each reading.

**5.** During rehearsal for your next speech, deliberately try to speak in as dull a voice as possible. Stifle all impulses to gesture. Then practice speaking with as colorful a voice as possible, giving full freedom to movement and gesture. Notice how a colorful and expressive presentation makes your ideas seem more lively and vivid as you speak.

**Comments:** Students may try the exercise in front of a full-length mirror, to gauge their eye contact and facial expressions. Audiotaping the assignment can also be revealing. Does the first version sound significantly different from the second (which attempts to use maximum variety)?

**6.** Form groups of five students and conduct an impromptu speaking contest. Each participant should supply two topics for impromptu speaches, and participants should then draw two topics (not their own). Participants have 15 minutes to prepare a three-minute speech on one of these topics. Each student should present the speech to the group, which selects a winner.

**Comments:** You may wish to give suggestions on the types of topics: one word, common saying, quotation, current interest. Discuss: What preparation strategies did you use during the 15 minutes? What criteria did you use to select the best speaker?

## VOICE AND APPEARANCE CHECK LIST

Check each characteristic that applies to the speaker's presence.

| | |
|---|---|
| _____ breathiness in voice | _____ little, hidden gestures |
| _____ thin voice | _____ conversational gestures |
| _____ flat vocal quality | _____ repetitive gestures |
| _____ nasal voice | _____ rhythmic gestures |
| _____ throatiness | _____ distracting habits |
| _____ rounded vowels | _____ paces while speaking |
| _____ fast rate | _____ rocks on feet |
| _____ slow rate | _____ pounds/taps podium |
| _____ high pitch | _____ moves to show emphasis |
| _____ soft voice | _____ clothes enhance presentation |
| _____ loud voice | _____ attire overwhelms the speech |
| _____ animated facial expressions | _____ looks prepared |
| _____ deep voice | _____ shuffles, plays with notes |
| _____ colorful vocal variety | _____ leaves podium before last word |
| _____ smiles frequently | _____ ums, ers, you knows, uhs |
| _____ poker face | _____ really cares |
| _____ eye contact with audience | _____ likes the audience |
| _____ avoids eye contact | _____ looks tense |
| _____ uses grand gestures | |

# ADDITIONAL EXERCISES

## PHONE-ANSWERING-MACHINE MESSAGE

**Purpose:** To analyze vocal qualities on a mediated channel

**Procedures:**

1. Secure access to a phone-answering machine and attach it to your office phone. (Be sure the machine will record up to thirty minutes.)

2. Ask each student to leave a brief (30-60-second) message on the machine, using descriptive language on a topic of recent interest. The student should state his or her name at the end of the message. Alternative assignment: Ask each student to call and read the same message.

   When making this assignment, offer students a sample message, such as: "Hi. I'm calling to tell you about an exciting opportunity to travel during the next holiday. If you're in the spirit to get going and quit grading those papers, let me know. This is _____ from _____."

   Post the hours when students may call and distribute the phone number.

3. Play the message-filled tape in class. Instruct students to make notes on: Which messages were easiest to listen to? Why? What is noticeable about pitch, loudness, enunciation, pronunciation, and so on? What are common mispronunciations? How much vocal variety is necessary to be interesting on this medium?

## VOCAL VARIETY AND LOUDNESS PRACTICE

**Purpose:** To practice vocal variety and loudness

**Procedures:**

1. Prepare a grab bag of empty cartons, wrappers, containers, and objects with writing on them (toothpaste box, junk mail, and so on).

2. Bring the grab bag to class and have the first student select an item.

3. Tell the student to read the content, using one of the emotions/qualities listed below. (You can make this into a game by putting the words below on index cards and having students draw both an item from the grab bag and a card.) The student must read the content of the item, using the given emotion/quality. If the first reading is not acceptable, ask the class to help by coaching: What do people do when they express anger? Sadness? . . .

- Anger
- Sadness
- Sexiness
- Boredom
- Happiness
- Pomposity
- Instructiveness
- Contentment
- Excitement

4. Repeat the process with a second student and a different item and emotion/quality.

5. Discuss: What vocal elements do we alter to convey different feelings?

## IMPROMPTU SPEECH: MINI-LESSON AND TOPICS

**Purpose:** To practice preparing an impromptu speech

**Procedures:** Competitive impromptu speakers often use the following method to help them quickly organize a speech. In a situation in which they draw three possible topics, the speakers follow these steps:

1. Draw the topics and read them. Discard any you don't understand. Select one quickly.

2. Try to "free-associate" with the topic to find areas you can speak on. If the topic is "It is better to suffer evil than to do evil," associations might include: the nature of good and evil, the value of suffering, people who have suffered great evil but been good, Plato's philosophy of rhetoric.

3. Select one association to serve as the theme of your speech. Write it down on an index card.

4. Select two to four areas to discuss under the theme (the main points). Write down a word to remind you of each area. The main points usually fall naturally into one of the following organizational patterns: categorical; past, present, future; problem-solution; cause-effect.

5. Think of a story, example, personal experience, or explanatory detail under each main point. Jot down a word to remind you of the content of each.

6. Think of a story, example, personal experience, fable, or quotation to use as the introduction.

7. Check your notes. Begin speaking.

8. This system of impromptu speaking works because good impromptu speakers have a solid grasp of organizational design (step 4 above) and understand the functions of the parts of a speech (the introduction, body, conclusion, and so on). Consequently, the speaker automatically knows to include these parts in the speech without making notations about them on the card. When presented, the speech will include:

   a. An interesting introduction that gets attention

   b. A link between the introduction and the topic, followed by a statement about the topic selected

   c. A link between the topic and theme

   d. A statement about the theme's significance or relevance to the topic. What can the audience learn?

   e. A preview of the main points

   f. A discussion of each main point, using a narrative or example for each

   g. A review or summary of the main points

   h. Either a recap of the topic or a reference to the introduction to function as closure

## Sets of Three Possible Impromptu Topics:

1. Taxation with representation isn't so hot, either.
2. What's the new American dream?
3. There's a computer in your future.

1. Let sleeping dogs lie.
2. We are the servants, not the masters, of technology.
3. "It's time to speak," the Walrus said. . . .

1. Kilroy was here.
2. To dream the impossible dream . . .
3. "From shadows and symbols into truth." (John Henry)

1. A bird in the hand . . .
2. "Tell me not in mournful numbers, life is but an empty dream. . . ." (Longfellow)
3. "Wisdom grows by taking pains." (Cato)

1. "Nature has given man one tongue and two ears that we may hear twice as much as we speak." (Epictetus)
2. "Life and misery begin together." (Fuller)
3. An apple a day . . .

1. "Meanness is the parent of insolence." (Franklin)
2. "That's one small step for a man, one giant step for mankind." (Armstrong)
3. He's the toast of the town.

1. Thanks, for what?
2. Rocky mountain high
3. "Words are but words." (Beaumont and Fletcher)

1. When push comes to shove . . .
2. "Courage without conscience is a wild beast." (Ingersoll)
3. When in doubt, mumble; when in trouble, delegate; when in charge, ponder.

## ADDITIONAL RESOURCES

Anderson, Virgil A. *Training the Speaking Voice*, 3rd ed. (New York: Oxford University Press, 1977).

Bytwerk, Randall L. "Impromptu Speaking Exercise." *Communication Education* 34 (April 1985): 148–149.

Eakins, Barbara W., and R. Gene Eakins. *Sex Differences in Human Communication* (Boston: Houghton Mifflin Co., 1978).

Eisenson, Jon. *Voice and Diction: A Program for Improvement*, 5th ed. (New York: Macmillan, 1985).

Hall, Judith A. "Voice Tone and Persuasion." *Journal of Personality and Social Psychology* 38 (June 1980): 924–936.

Knapp, Mark L. *Essentials of Nonverbal Communication* (New York: Holt Rinehart and Winston, 1980).

Pearson, Judy C. *Gender and Communication* (Dubuque, Iowa: Wm. C. Brown, 1985).

"Communicating Correctly." McGraw-Hill (1969). 16 minutes.

"Communication by Voice and Action." Centron Films. 14 minutes.

"Communication: The Nonverbal Agenda." CRM/McGraw-Hill. 30 minutes.

"Improve Your Pronunciation." Coronet. 11 minutes.

# 11

## The Nature and Kinds of Informative Speaking

## CHAPTER OBJECTIVES

After reading Chapter 11, students should be able to:

1. Name and differentiate among the three functions of an informative speech.

2. Understand the relationship between informative speaking and learning.

3. Use techniques to attract and sustain attention.

4. Select an appropriate design for an informative speech.

## DISCUSSION (TEXT P. 310)

1. Analyze Juli Pardell's speech in Appendix B of this book in terms of its function, type, and design. Discuss how it arouses and holds attention and motivates learning. Can you think of a different or better design for the speech?

**Comments:** The major function of Ms. Pardell's speech is to share information on air traffic problems with her audience. A secondary function would be to shape the perceptions of the audience concerning such problems. In fulfilling this secondary function we would be predisposing the audience for later persuasive communications on the topic. This speech is a speech of explanation in that it describes the major problems involved in air traffic control and discusses the origins of these problems. The design of the speech is a combined design. The major structural design is categorical, but a causation design is used within the categories. Ms. Pardell arouses and holds attention through her use of examples. She motivates the audience to learn by relating the topic to travel over the spring break, bringing it clearly into the realm of audience relevance. Alternative design structures which would have been effective include an historical design which focused on air safety problems and a comparison and contrast design that compared air travel safety with safety problems on other means of public transportation.

2. Select your nominations for the "best" and "worst" lecturers you have as instructors this semester, excluding your speech instructor. Without naming these individuals, discuss how they design their presentations and encourage or discourage learning in their classes.

**Comments:** Ask the following questions: Can you tell what is going to happen on that day from the instructors' opening remarks? How are the lectures organized? Are clear transitions provided from point to point? Do the professors preview the day's lecture? How would you classify the lectures as kinds of informative speeches? Which six factors of attention/retention are used by your instructors? During the discussion, you may wish to encourage students to differentiate between their like/dislike for the material and each instructor's attempts to make it relevant to the audience.

3. Discuss the relationship between information and power. Give specific examples of the use and misuse of such power.

**Comments:** A variety of avenues are open for discussion. Students may specify examples of interpersonal misuses of information (the misuse of information given in trust); the imbalance of information in employer-employee relations (for example, a wealth of information is available to supervisors about subordinates, but a dearth of information is available to subordinates about supervisors); or education itself as a kind of information power. What salespeople tell and don't tell about their products is a kind of information power ("The car has only 40,000 miles on it"—of course, they were all on rough gravel roads); what politicians reveal and conceal is a kind of information power (is "executive privilege" a way of misusing the power to conceal information?); and access to computers and information networks is a kind of information power. You may wish to direct students' attention to certain arenas for discussion, such as politics (national, interoffice, interpersonal).

## APPLICATION (TEXT PP. 310–311)

**1.** Select an informative topic, determine a specific purpose, and outline the main points in the order in which you would present them, using at least two of the following designs:

a. spatial

b. analogy

c. categorical

d. sequential

For each design, explain how you would motivate listeners to learn.

**Comments:** To motivate listeners, students can focus on the questions: Why should listeners care about my topic? How might listeners use this information? Any topic offers a variety of opportunities to motivate listeners. For each of the above designs, a topic well-suited to the design is offered, plus reasons that might motivate listeners to learn about the topic.

(a) spatial: The Path Followed by Lewis and Clark. Listeners might visit the Pacific Northwest and trace part of the path followed by Lewis and Clark. They might obtain a better understanding of the geography of a part of the United States. They might better understand how and why the Pacific Northwest was settled.

(b) analogy: The Educational Marathon—Establishing a Summer Training Program. Listeners could personally benefit from getting ahead before the academic year starts. They might get better grades. They might not have to study so hard during the year and might have more time for sports, work, or recreation. Parents may wish these benefits for their children.

(c) categorical: Hardward, Software, and Peripherals—What's a Computer All About? Listeners could better understand the workings of the machine that is changing the work place. They might purchase a computer and need to know how to talk to salespeople.

(d) sequential: The Development of the Modern Typewriter. Listeners could better understand how grateful they should be for self-correcting typewriters and easy-to-use keyboards. They could understand why the keys are placed as they are on a keyboard. Their curiosity about how the invention was developed could be satisfied.

**2.** Plan the informative speech you prepare for class to be sure you use at least three of the six factors of attention: intensity, repetition, novelty, activity, contrast, and relevance. Turn in a short statement specifying the techniques you will use and why you believe they will be effective.

**Comments:** This exercise could be done as a group activity. Instruct students to bring to class five copies of their initial outlines for the next speech. Have students analyze them to identify the factors of attention they use. Students can help each other locate placed in the speeches where an attention device would be useful.

# ADDITIONAL EXERCISES

## WHY SHOULD I CARE? AN EXERCISE IN DETERMINING RELEVANCE

**Purpose:** To practice selecting motivational appeals to induce listeners to see a topic as relevant and significant

**Procedures:**

1. You can use this exercise as a group task in class or as an individual homework assignment. Instruct students to determine what appeals they would make to invite each audience below to listen to topic 1. Repeat the process for topics 2 and 3.

| Topics | Audiences |
|---|---|
| 1. Automobile safety | a. General audience |
| 2. Bicycling vacations | b. Speech class |
| 3. Water conservation | c. Farmers |

2. Discuss: How did you alter the appeals on the same topic, depending on which audience would receive the message? Are there some appeals that apply to everyone, and others that are audience-specific? How important is it to give an audience a reason to care about your topic?

## ARENAS OF INFORMATIVE SPEECH

**Purpose:** To discover how often speakers give informative speeches

**Procedures:**

1. Divide the class into work groups. Instruct each group to write down common examples of places/occasions where people (businesspeople, teachers, students, newspeople, and so on) give informative speeches. Which of these speeches are speeches of description, demonstration, or explanation?

2. Request each group to report on their list.

3. Discuss: How often do we use the skill of informative speaking in our society? Do we use one type of informative speech (demonstration, description, or explanation) more than another?

## DEMONSTRATION SPEECH SKILLS

**Purpose:** To examine special skills for speeches of demonstration

**Procedures:**

1. Assign students to work groups. Instruct them to investigate how visual aids are used in speeches of demonstration. They may consult other speech texts, observe salespeople, or interview speakers. The group should prepare both a written and an oral report entitled "The Dos and Don'ts of Demonstrations."

2. Request each group to report orally. Note: A wide variety of answers will be produced. The intent is to stimulate thought about how the preparation, practice, and implementation of this type of informative speech differs from the other types'. Dos will include items like practice with the material before the actual speech, use models and simulations when the object itself is cumbersome, avoid dead air while you are demonstrating, work extra hard for eye contact while demonstrating, have several aids showing the completed steps in the process being demonstrated, display the product with the label toward the audience, and so on.

3. Discuss: Does a speech of demonstration require different preparation than other types of informative speeches? Do most of the people you have seen follow the suggestions made by the class? What are the most common errors?

## ADDITIONAL RESOURCES

Frandsen, Kenneth D., and Donald A. Clement. "The Functions of Human Communication in Informing: Communicating and Processing Information." In *Handbook of Rhetorical and Communication Theory*, Carroll C. Arnold and John Waite Bowers, ed. (Boston: Allyn and Bacon, 1984).

Petrie, Charles. "Informative Speaking: A Summary and Bibliography of Related Research." *Speech Monographs* 30 (June 1963): 79–91.

"Information Processing." CRM Production. 29 minutes.

"Types of Information." Films for the Humanities. 15 minutes.

# 12

## The Use of Supporting Materials

## CHAPTER OBJECTIVES

After reading Chapter 12, students should be able to:

1. Select the appropriate combination of supporting materials for a speech.

2. Evaluate the different types of supporting materials used in other speakers' presentations, using the appropriate criteria.

3. Translate statistical data into information an audience can relate to and comprehend.

4. Understand the value of examples and use them effectively as support in a speech.

5. Understand the importance of narratives and be able to use them effectively as supports in a speech.

6. Identify and distinguish among the different types of testimony and their functions.

# DISCUSSION (TEXT P. 337)

**1.** Evaluate the use of testimony in two of the student speeches in Appendix B of this book. What types of testimony are used? Are they appropriate to the purpose? Do the speakers introduce source qualifications?

**Comments:** What examples were found of lay testimony? Did the testimony fit the criteria for appropriate use of lay testimony? If it were used incorrectly, how would the speaker have to alter the reference to be ethical or correct? Repeat the same questions with expert testimony and prestige testimony.

Further discussion can focus on: Do I know enough about the experts to know if they are unbiased? What potency does lay or prestige testimony have as logical proof or as emotional proof?

**2.** President Reagan is known as a speaker who uses narrative very effectively. Find examples of the President's speeches in the *Weekly Compilation of Presidential Documents* and study his use of narrative as supporting material. Does narrative perform a vital purpose for him? Does he rely too heavily or too little on it? If so, how does this weaken his speeches?

**Comments:** You may wish to require students to duplicate the page(s) from a Reagan speech that contains a narrative and to write their analyses on the back(s) of the page(s).

Generally, Reagan seems to use examples and narratives more than other recent Presidents. These techniques function to emotionally connect him with the audience and to enliven or authenticate his claims. His use of examples and narratives is most effective in ceremonial speeches. In persuasive speeches, when the examples or narratives are not ties to other proofs, the overall strength is weakened. His overuse of examples and narratives in these speeches may weaken his believability for those who are undecided about an issue.

**3.** Select a speech from a recent issue of *Vital Speeches of the Day* that uses statistical information for support. What kind of statistics are used? Are they used effectively? Did the speaker supplement the statistical information with examples? Share your analysis with your classmates.

**Comments:** Ask students to duplicate the speech and underline the statistics, labeling each type of statistic in the margin. Have students evaluate the statistics on a separate sheet of paper.

Discuss: Statistics may be descriptive or inferential. Students may also find examples of implied statistics ("More doctors recommend Bayer"). What makes statistics effective in the examples students located? What makes statistics boring and ineffective? What forms of proof are statistics paired with (example, testimony, narrative)? If you had to give three tips of advice about using statistics to a beginning speaker, what would they be?

**4.** Look in newspapers or magazines for recent public statements by government officials that purport to be factual but that actually contain a high degree of distortion. What tips you off to the distortion? Would most people be likely to detect this bias?

**Comments:** This assignment can be particularly fun if students also look for bias in newspapers like *The Star* or the *National Enquirer*. These papers often contain several levels of bias—pseudo-expert testimony, unbelievable statistics, and misleading headlines. This type of distortion can also be found in numerous other sources—letters to the editor and student newspapers, for example.

Government officials often distort by simplification, labeling, and euphemisms (words that sanitize objectionable acts or concepts—for instance, "pacification" of Vietnamese villages means wiping them out.

This assignment can lead to fruitful discussions about the consumer-protection value of studying public speaking. With training we become more critical and analytical in our consumption of messages.

# APPLICATION (TEXT PP. 337–338)

**1.** Develop a hypothetical example or narrative to illustrate one of the following abstract concepts:

love
compassion
charity
welfare
justice

**Comments:** Sometimes these narratives will be stories with a moral or punch line that links to the concept or point. Former Idaho Senator Frank Church, Chairman of the Senate Foreign Relations Committee and Special Committee to Investigate Abuse of Covert Activities in the 1970s, often used narratives in his introductions to link to the theme of his speeches. One of the most potent examples of his narratives was a dramatized version of an actual occurrence. This narrative often occurred in the middle of his speeches about the errors of our foreign policy and covert activities.

"Bethine [his wife] and I keep a little cabin up in the hills not far from Gettysburg in Pennsylvania, up in that beautiful Pennsylvania-Dutch countryside. We go there on weekends to escape Washington. We've done it for years. We love that beautifully kept country, the honesty of the people—too many Republicans, actually; rather like Idaho in that respect. One of them is the egg farmer we get our eggs from. Of course, it's that arrangement where you go to the back porch, the eggs are there, you put in whatever money into a little slot and take the eggs you want to take. And in all the years that I had been there the farmer had never come to see me, which was one of the reasons I suspected he was Republican. But on this particular day, I got out of the car, and I know that he had asked his wife to watch for us because she evidently had seen us approaching through the kitchen window and she'd picked up the telephone and called him at the hen house. By the time I came back to my car with the eggs he was there in front of me. And he was a big man, and he was in overalls, and I didn't know quite what to expect. So I held the eggs up between us. . . . And he said, 'Senator, I want to ask you a question.' And I said, 'What is it?' And he said, 'I want to know whether or not it's true that my government has been mixing with the Mafia for the purpose of murdering people.' And I said 'Yes, I must tell you that that is true.' And I could've hit him with my hand, such as was the visible effect of those words on his face, his expression. He stepped back and with his boot he kicked the dirt a few times and didn't know quite what to say. And then he looked at me and he said, 'Senator, how are we going to teach our children to grow up honest if their government is in bed with the Mafia?'

That's how far we came. And we paid a terrible penalty for that period in which the moral content of government decision-making was subordinated to all the pragmatic attitudes of the time." (From a speech at Temple Beth Shobar on January 23, 1977. Printed with permission of the Frank Church Collection, Boise State University, Boise, Idaho.)

Discussion should focus on how this narrative uses humor to lead into the seriousness of the point, uses concrete detail in describing the place and people, and draws a moral about the times.

**2.** Note how television advertisements often use facts and figures, examples, narratives, or testimony in combination with visual aids. Analyze and evaluate a current television advertisement with respect to these techniques, using the criteria provided in this chapter.

**Comments:** The movie *Promises* spoofs several misleading devices used in television advertisements and would be a good warm-up for this exercise.

**3.** Determine which types of testimony might best support the following statements:

a. Recent NCAA rulings are unfair to black athletes.

b. Campus security measures are inadequate.

c. Teenage pregnancy is a national disaster.

    d. Soviet-American relations have taken a turn for the better.

    e. The proper diet can help prevent cancer.

    f. Asian immigrant children are outperforming their American-born counterparts in public schools.

    g. Religious training is often an important part of a child's development.

    h. Sororities perform an important function on our campus.

**Comments:**
    (a) Expert testimony from objective sources; lay testimony
    (b) Lay testimony from a victim of the inadequacy; expert testimony about increasing crime rates
    (c) Expert or lay testimony
    (d) Expert testimony from political scientists; prestige testimony from a world leader
    (e) Expert testimony
    (f) Expert testimony
    (g) Expert testimony
    (h) Lay testimony

# ADDITIONAL EXERCISES

## WHAT'S WRONG WITH THE SUPPORTING MATERIAL?

**Purpose:** To examine common misuses of supporting material

**Procedures:**

1. Have students, individually or in groups, look for errors in the use of supporting materials in informative speeches, advertisements, or magazine articles.

2. Discuss: What is the error? How often do you find this kind of mistake? What kinds of questions can you ask to clarify if supporting material is reliable?

## TRANSLATING STATISTICS

**Purpose:** To help students learn to state statistics in understandable ways

**Procedure:**

1. Use this exercise as an individual homework assignment or task in class. Duplicate the statistics from the Additional Exercise, "Visual Aid Presentation of Statistics," in Chapter 8 of this *Guide* (excluding item (e), which contains translated statistics).

2. Instruct students to translate these statistics in ways that would make them more understandable for an audience.

3. Discuss: What strategies did you use when translating the statistics? What information is lost when statistics are translated?

## RHETORICAL EXAMPLE PRACTICE

**Purpose:** To practice creating rhetorical examples

**Procedures:**

1. Use this exercise as an individual homework assignment or as a group task in class. Ask students to create a rhetorical example to fit each of the following:

   **a.** Thousands die yearly from not being buckled.

   **b.** Hundreds of thousands of hungry live and die in developing nations.

   **c.** As many as 100,000 high school students debate each year.

   **d.** Thousands of unwed teens become pregnant yearly.

   **e.** Hundreds of farmers lost their land to foreclosure.

2. Have each student or group share a rhetorical example of the first topic. Instruct students to jot down notes on their favorite examples. After discussing the first subject, repeat the procedure for the remaining subjects.

3. Discuss: What techniques were the most effective? What sets them apart from the rest? What cautions do you need to remember when using these techniques in your speeches? In the class discussion, you may want to caution students that the rhetorical example must be in keeping with facts, not overdramatized.

## ADDITIONAL RESOURCES

Kellerman, Kathy. "The Concept of Evidence: A Critical Review." *Journal of the American Forensics Association* 16 (1980): 159–172.

Newman, Robert, and Dale Newman. *Evidence* (Boston: Houghton Mifflin Co., 1969).

Reynolds, Rodney A., and Michael Bergoon. "Belief Processing, Reasoning, and Evidence." In *Communication Yearbook 7*, Robert N. Bostrom, ed. (Beverly Hills, Calif.: Sage Publications, 1983).

Yalch, R. E., and R. Elmore-Yalch. "The Effective Numbers on the Route to Persuasion." *Journal of Consumer Research* 11 (June 1984): 522–527.

"Killing Us Softly: The Images of Women in Advertising." CAMDF. 30 minutes.

"Promises." RAM Film. 21 minutes.

# 13

## The Nature and Kinds of Persuasive Speaking

## CHAPTER OBJECTIVES

After reading this chapter, students should be able to:

1. Compare the characteristics of informative and persuasive speaking.

2. Understand McGuire's model of the persuasive process.

3. Utilize the techniques to remove listeners' barriers to commitment.

4. Differentiate among the three types of persuasive speeches and select the appropriate type for a specific purpose.

5. Use the four organizational designs especially well-suited for persuasive speeches.

# DISCUSSION (TEXT P. 367)

**1.** Examine magazine advertisements and newspaper articles for examples of persuasion cloaked as information. What alerts you to the persuasive intent? In what respect does such pseudo-information possess the characteristics of persuasion discussed in this chapter? In what respects does it possess the characteristics of informative discourse discussed in Chapter 11?

**Comments:** Numerous examples abound of producers who "inform" us of the wonders of their products or of the propensity of events ("You have bad breath more often than you think"). The factor that usually alerts us to the persuasive intent is that the advertiser wants something from us—donations, purchases, attitude change. Most of the elements discussed under "The Process of Persuasion" section will apply to the advertisements examined by students. The elements of information are the cloak that gets our attention and hides the persuasive appeal.

As an extended assignment, you could ask students to duplicate or copy a pseudo-informative advertisement and bring it to class.

**2.** The letters to the editor section of the Sunday newspaper is often a rich (and raw!) source for the study of persuasive material. Using a recent Sunday paper, analyze the persuasion attempted in these letters. Which do you think are most and least effective, and why?

**Comments:** Letters to the editor are the perfect source for fallacies discussed in the next chapter. You may be able to reuse the letters collected for this assignment for Chapter 14.

Students will find a wide variety of persuasive attempts, from reasonable argumentation to wild and illogical ravings. You may wish to have students examine the letters for: organizational design, refutation, specific appeals, use of evidence, or multi- versus singlesided presentations. Are rational, organized letters more persuasive than letters that use other strategies?

**3.** The speech on responsible drinking and driving which appears at the end of this chapter was prepared for a college student audience. What changes would you suggest in this speech if it were to be presented to a luncheon meeting of the Women's Christian Temperance Union? Why?

**Comments:** This question directs students' attention back to basic audience analysis and determination of audience attitudes toward the subject. The new group is anti-alcohol and presumably would have rigid attitudes about drinking. The prior attitudes of this audience change the place in the persuasion process where the speaker starts (the audience accepts the fact that drinking is bad). Audience attitudes also change the role the speaker can cast the audience in—the student-oriented speech presumed the audience drinks and cast them in the role of potential offenders. The "we" pronoun when referring to drinkers would be inappropriate for the new audience and credibility-robbing for the speaker.

**4.** When should a speaker give up trying to persuade a hostile audience and simply confront listeners directly with the position they oppose? Why would a speaker bother to do this? Might speaker and audience gain anything from such a confrontation? Can you find an example of such a speech? Do you agree with the strategy it used? Discuss it in class.

**Comments:** Generally, speakers wish to attempt incremental softening of opinion with hostile audiences and to save their credibility for later persuasive attempts. Hence, confrontation will only occur as a last resort. An exception to this occurs when only a portion of the audience is hostile and confronting that portion of the audience can be used to motivate the partisans to action. Attacking the opinions of one group can polarize and alienate them from the portions of the audience the speaker has targeted. The technique is perilous and fraught with ethical pitfalls. Examples of polarization can be found in many of George Wallace's presidential campaign speeches of the 1960s.

# APPLICATION (TEXT P. 368)

**1.** Keep a diary of your day, identifying all the moments in which you confront and practice persuasion. Evaluate your adventure in persuasion. When were you most and least persuaded, and most and least persuasive? Why? Did you encounter (or commit!) any ethical abuses?

**Comments:** A variety of experiences will be reported as you lead discussion of the diary assignment. Initially, students have a presumption that they are not exposed to much persuasion. This assignment may be a vehicle for convincing them of the pervasiveness of persuasion and the need for classes like this one to empower the consumer with defenses against unwanted persuasion.

**2.** Read "The Gift of Life" by Paul B. Fowler in Appendix B and identify the following:

a. the challenge the speaker confronted

b. the type of persuasive speech

c. the design of the speech

Analyze the speech using the McGuire model of the persuasive process.

**Comments:** This application may be assigned in class or as a homework assignment. The answers should contain at least the following information:

a. The challenge Mr. Fowler faced was moving an apathetic audience to action. While most people favor organ donations for transplants, few take the time to sign an organ donor card or lobby their representatives for better funding or improved communication systems. Mr. Fowler met this challenge by the technique referred to in the text (pp. 355–356), justifying action. He uses examples to present vivid images of need.

b. The speech is a speech urging action and he spells out the consequences of inaction, thus providing compelling reasons to overcome caution or apathy.

c. The design is essentially a problem-solution design (as noted in the introduction to the speech) but Mr. Fowler also considers two categories of problems as well: problems of funding and problems of communication.

In terms of the McGuire model, Mr. Fowler opens with audience-involving examples that gain the attention of his listeners (reception phase). Next, he orients the audience by providing understandable information about the problem that should also increase the saliency for the audience. Since agreement is probably not at issue, he then moves to the integration phase in the McGuire model with a call for action from the audience.

**3.** Select a controversial subject and outline the types of persuasive speech you would present to:

a. an uncommitted audience

b. an audience in agreement

c. an audience in opposition

Discuss the differences among your approaches.

**Comments:** Subject example: Schools should be able to post the Ten Commandments.

(a) Uncommitted audiences must first be educated about the problem, then persuaded that it affects them personally in some fashion, and finally, persuaded to take the action recommended by the speaker. Note that all of these steps may not occur in the same message.

(b) An audience in agreement may be reminded of the facts, if necessary, to renew their commitment. However, the primary emphasis should be an appeal urging them to action.

(c) An audience in opposition must be treated as a hostile audience. The speaker must spend the majority of the speech creating identification with the audience and developing common goals and values.

**4.** A public forum is being held on campus on the issue of drinking and driving. The first speaker on the program is Betty Nichols, who will present the speech included at the end of this chapter. You have been asked to refute her position. Outline the speech you will present.

**Comments:** This assignment works well as a group activity. Answers should follow the five steps recommended for developing an effective refutation. Possible points of refutation include: Nichols's emotional representation of the facts and trying to frighten the audience; her assumption that the audience is not responsible; her specific reasons why the problem exists; her implied threats of what happens legally to those who drive under the influence; or the premise that she has the right problem but the wrong solution.

# ADDITIONAL EXERCISES

## RHETORICAL OBSTACLES

**Purpose:** To identify the barriers in topics and situations

**Procedures:**

1. Explain the concept of rhetorical obstacles to the class. Rhetorical obstacles are barriers inherent in the situation, speaker ethos, or audience attitudes that can be altered by language. While a power outage that leaves the audience in complete darkness is an obstacle to persuasion, it is not necessarily a rhetorical obstacle.

2. In groups, assign students to discover the rhetorical obstacles inherent in each of the following problems. What strategy would they recommend to overcome the obstacles?

   **a.** Your topic is AIDS.

   **b.** You must defend yourself before the university judiciary.

   **c.** You must request money from a group that feels unappreciated by past recipients.

   **d.** You must respond to a letter questioning why the YWCA lets devil-promoting, new age classes be held in its building.

   **e.** You must talk to a group of employees about listening. The employees were told by their boss that they must attend the workshop, in the hope that it might do them some good.

3. Discuss: What obstacles were found in each problem? Did different groups find the same obstacles? What are the two most immediate problems? How would you begin to overcome them? How important is locating rhetorical obstacles to your probable persuasive success?

## ADDITIONAL RESOURCES

Boster, F. J., and P. Mongeau. "Fear-Arousing Persuasive Messages." In *Communication Yearbook* 8, R. N. Bostrom and B. H. Westley, ed. (Beverly Hills, Calif.: Sage Publications, 1984).

Bozik, Mary. "An Exercise in Inference Making." *Communication Education* 33 (October 1984): 401–403.

Burgoon, M., J. P. Dilard, and N. E. Doran. "Friendly and Unfriendly Persuasion: The Effects of Violations of Expectations by Males and Females." *Human Communication Research* 19 (Winter 1983): 283–294.

Fritz, Paul A., and Richard L. Weaver II. "Teaching Critical Thinking Skills in the Public Speaking Course: A Liberal Arts Perspective." *Communication Education* 35 (April 1986). 174–181.

Gruner, Charles. "Advice to the Beginning Speaker on Using Humor—What the Research Tells Us." *Communication Education* 34 (April 1985): 142–147.

Jenson, Keith, and David A. Carter. "Self-Persuasion: The Effects of Public Speaking on Speakers." *Southern Speech Communication Journal* (Winter 1981): 163–174.

Simons, Herbert W. *Persuasion: Understanding, Practice and Analysis*, 2nd ed. (New York: Random House, 1986).

Smith, Mary John. *Persuasion and Human Action: A Review and Critique of Social Influence Theories* (Belmont, Calif.: Wadsworth Publishing Co., 1982).

# 14

# Evidence, Proof, and Argument

## CHAPTER OBJECTIVES

After reading this chapter, students should be able to:

1. Use evidence and proofs effectively in a speech.

2. Understand the meaning and function of different types of proof.

3. Explain the two forms of reasoned argument: inductive and deductive reasoning.

4. Use and differentiate among the major forms of argument.

5. Identify defective evidence, proof, and argument--in their own and others' speeches.

# DISCUSSION (TEXT PP. 400–401)

**1.** Study the use of narrative as evidence in Elie Wiesel's "Nobel Prize Acceptance Speech" in Appendix B. Is it probable that this narrative created identification among speaker, audience, and subject? Does language play a crucial role in its effectiveness? Does the speaker use dialogue effectively? Does the narrative generate proof by mythos? How?

**Comments:** The body of Mr. Wiesel's acceptance speech is an extended narrative based on an imagined conversation between himself as an adult and himself as a young boy who experienced the horrors of the Holocaust. The use of this unusual autobiographical dialogue provides the audience with a sense of closeness to the situation being described. It is as though they were eyewitnesses to the action and anguish, able to experience and share the feelings of the participants. When Mr. Wiesel speaks of the "young Jewish boy discovering the Kingdom of Night," he draws on the archetypal metaphor of light and darkness. As was noted in Chapter 9, archetypal metaphors are a powerful means of arousing common feelings and uniting diverse audiences because they involve the constants of human experiences and sensibilities. The narratives of the young boy experiencing the kingdom of night, and emerging from it to work for world peace and the betterment of all mankind, also evokes the rebirth archetype which lends an aura of faith and hope to this moving speech. The eloquence of Mr. Wiesel's language contributes to the effectiveness of this address. For example, his use of personification, antithesis, and parallel construction in the sentences "Neutrality helps the oppressor, never the victim. Silence encourages the tormentor, never the tormented." makes them especially memorable and moving. Although this is a ceremonial speech, it has persuasive overtones. You can help students to see how some of the techniques employed here work equally well for persuasive speeches.

**2.** Find examples of effective and ineffective uses of testimony in the student speeches in Appendix B of this book. Are the sources carefully documented? Are expert, prestige, and lay forms of testimony used appropriately? How might these forms have been used more effectively?

**Comments:** "The Right Fuel" contains no testimony. Expert testimony would have served as additional proof for Ms. Taylor's claims about nutrition. Although her personal credibility was strong on this topic, expert testimony would have made the claims even mo: credible. Expert testimony would have enhanced the identification within the speech.

"Are the Skies That Friendly?" relies primarily on expert testimony from newspapers and magazines (*Time, U.S. News & World Report, Christian Science Monitor*). Discuss: Are the magazines and newspapers quoted the best sources on the topic? Are dates given to show the currency of the information? How could lay testimony add to this speech?

"The Gift of Life" uses a mixture of types of testimony. Several books, a Gallup poll, and a professional journal provide expert testimony. The examples which open and end the speech serve as lay testimony. Discuss: Are these the best sources? Are you given enough information to evaluate the sources of the information and when the testimony was given? Are books better sources than professional journals? The end of the speech uses lay testimony quoted from a journal. Does the lay testimony make the topic more personal?

3. Find examples of admirable, desirable, and obligatory good reasons in the speeches in Appendix B. Under what conditions might each type be most effective?

**Comments:** "The Right Fuel" uses desirable (good for self) reasons.

"Are the Skies That Friendly?" uses desirable and obligatory good reasons (we should pressure for safer travel because it may be beneficial to self and others and is the right thing to do).

"The Gift of Life" uses desirable (for the good of all and perhaps for me personally), admirable (it is good to provide the opportunity for a normal life), and obligatory (we owe it to others to become donors) good reasons.

Discuss: When is each of these good reasons most effective—in terms of relevance, consequences, and consistency?

4. Bring to class examples of magazine and newspaper ads that demonstrate the four basic types of persuasive proof: logos, pathos, ethos, and mythos. Discuss how these proofs are used and why you think they are or are not effective.

**Comments:** You may wish to procure advertisements for use with this exercise. Does one type of advertisement seem more popular (or more easily chosen by students) than the others? You may wish to make this a group activity. If so, assign students to small groups. Have each group select the most and least effective advertisement from one type of proof. As each group reports, discuss what contributes to effectiveness or ineffectiveness. Ask students if they would have responded differently to the advertisements before studying this unit in the text.

5. Look for inductive and deductive forms of argument in the speeches in Appendix B. Do these arguments use units of proof adequately? Do they avoid fallacies?

**Comments:** The discussion question asks for three levels of analysis: (a) distinguishing between inductive and deductive reasoning, (b) judging the adequacy of proof, and (c) detecting fallacies. You may wish to assign the question as homework prior to discussion in class or to parcel the subsets of the question to different groups in class.

**6.** Look for examples of argument by perspective in the speeches in Appendix B. Do you think they are successful?

**Comments:** "The Right Fuel" builds an argument by perspective using analogy through the automobile maintenance comparison used throughout the speech.

**7.** Look for examples of misuse of evidence, proof, and argument in newspaper and magazine advertising. In your judgment, do these misuses reflect badly on the credibility of the product? Do the ads seem effective nonetheless?

**Comments:** Students should have no trouble finding cases of misuse of evidence. The advertisements reflect badly only if the audience is trained to detect the misuse. Discuss with students: When you know an advertisement misuses proof, do you refuse to buy the product or inform the president of the corporation?

**8.** Look for examples of defective persuasion in the letters to editor section of your local newspaper. Bring them to class for discussion.

**Comments:** Remind students to copy rather than rip out sections of the newspapers in the library. Letters to the editor are usually replete with fallacies. You may wish to ask students to identify the fallacies or reasoning errors in each of the letters they select. Other sources to find fallacies are argumentation textbooks (and accompanying instructor's manual). Several are listed under "Additional Resources" at the end of this chapter.

## APPLICATION (TEXT PP. 401–402)

**1.** Find a news story that interests you in the morning newspaper. Taking the information provided, (1) show how you might use this information as evidence in a persuasive speech, (2) structure a proof that would make use of this evidence, and (3) design an argument in which this proof might be critical.

**Comments:** This exercise requires three separate skills and will take some time and thought to grade. You may wish to require a copy of the news story along with the homework so you can check each student's choice of which segments to draw as evidence.

Stories may provide statistics, examples, lay testimony, prestige testimony, or expert testimony as evidence. In structuring a proof the student should provide a statement, evidence, claim, and qualifier, if needed. The argument should be a larger claim that the arrangement and contents of the proofs help support.

You may wish to go through one or two examples of the homework in class to help students (a) see how to build a unit of proof and (b) understand the relationship between single units of proof and an entire argument.

**2.** In *The Ethics of Rhetoric*, Richard Weaver observed that frequent arguments over the definitions of basic terms are a sign of division within a social group. Look for examples of public dispute over the definition of one of the following:

a. liberty

b. national defense

c. education

d. abortion

e. gun control

f. prayer in the school

g. peace

Do the contending arguments reflect the kind of social division Weaver suggested?

**Comments:** These arguments may be found in the head-to-head-issue segments of television shows, newspaper editorial pages, and magazine articles. Students may find titles in the *Reader's Guide to Periodical Literature* that suggest arguments over definition: "Prayer in School: Yes."

# ADDITIONAL EXERCISES

## FEAR APPEALS

**Purpose:** To identify fear appeals in advertisements

**Procedures:**

1. Instruct students to find an example of a fear appeal in a magazine advertisement, duplicate the advertisement, and bring it to class.

2. Have students take turns displaying their advertisements and explaining how the fear appeal functions in the advertisement.

3. Discuss: Are some fear appeals too strong, too subtle? How can fear appeals be used in public speaking? What cautions would you advise when using fear appeals? Can you think of examples of fear appeals that didn't work? (The movie *Reefer Madness* is a classic example of a failure.)

## PREPARING A PUBLIC SERVICE MESSAGE

**Purpose:**  To analyze the choices made in presenting public messages

**Procedure:**

1. Ask students to select an issue of local or national significance (blood donation or United Way, for example).

2. Tell students to suppose that they have been selected to create a brief (30-second) Public Service Message on the issue. The message should be persuasive, and thereby benefit the community.

3. Instruct students to write the Public Service Message, after carefully considering what strategy of argument they will use and what types of evidence will be most effective.

4. If possible, have students audiotape their messages and play the tapes during the next class session, or have students read their messages aloud.

5. After each message is presented, discuss: What strategy of argument was chosen? Was it effective? Does the class think another strategy may have been more effective? What type of evidence was utilized? Did it focus on ethos, pathos, logos, or mythos? Would other types or combinations of evidence have been more effective? Were fear appeals used? Were the fear appeals too strong?

# ADDITIONAL RESOURCES

---

Bozik, Mary. "An Exercise in Inference Making." *Communication Education* 33 (October 1984): 401–403.

Campbell, Karlyn Kohrs. *The Rhetorical Act* (Belmont, Calif.: Wadsworth Publishing Co., 1982). Chap. 9.

Ehninger, Douglas, and Gerard A. Hauser. "Communication of Values." In *Handbook of Rhetorical and Communication Theory*, Carroll C. Arnold and John Waite Bowers, ed. (Boston: Allyn and Bacon, 1984).

Jenson, J. Vernon. *Argumentation: Reasoning in Communication* (New York: D. Van Nostrand, 1981).

Rieke, Richard D., and Malcolm O. Sillars. *Argumentation and the Decision Making Process*, 2nd ed. (Glenview, Ill.: Scott, Foresman and Co., 1984).

Toulmin, Steven, Richard Rieke, and Allan Janik. *An Introduction to Reasoning*, 2nd ed. (New York: Macmillan Co., 1984).

Wilson, Barrie A. *The Anatomy of Argument*. (Lanham, Md.: University Press of America, 1980).

## SPECIAL FEATURE: CROSSWORD PUZZLE

**Directions:** Complete the crossword puzzle on the following page.

**Across**

1. One basis for argument
3. Bass
5. _____ conclusion
8. Fruit drink
9. Meaning of a term
10. Article of speech
12. Statistical probability
14. Not rich
17. Reasoning from the general to the specific
18. Twofold
19. _____ of the Mean
20. Supporting material
22. New York baseballer
23. Actual
24. Interpretations drawn from evidence

**Down**

1. Type of bread
2. Reasoning from the specific to the general
3. Tantrum
4. Slippery _____ fallacy
5. Cop
6. Name-calling attack
7. Plant's beginning
11. Arrangement of proofs and evidence
13. Not happy

14. Major or minor _____
15. Shady, diversionary technique
16. Error made by persuaders
20. Credibility
21. Final part of syllogism
24. Emotional appeal

**Across (cont.)**

27. Falsehood
29. Woman's name
31. Unquote (abbr.)
32. Egg _____
33. Rationality
36. Cry
37. _____ _____ *ergo propter hoc*
38. Connection to culture and tradition
40. _____ Rogers
41. Nautical yes

**Down (cont.)**

25. Basic pattern of deductive reasoning
26. It doesn't follow: *non* _____
28. Not out
29. Comparison
30. Not yes
34. Green light
35. Sad news section (abbr.)
38. Personal pronoun
39. Archaic you

# ANSWERS TO CHAPTER 14 PUZZLE

**Across**
1. reasoning
3. fish
5. hasty
8. ade
9. definition
10. the
12. odds
14. poor
17. deductive
18. dual
19. myth
20. evidence
22. Met
23. real
24. proofs
27. lie
29. Ann
31. unq
32. nog
33. logos
36. sob
37. post hoc
38. mythos
40. Roy
41. aye

**Down**
1. rye
2. inductive
3. fit
4. slope
5. hat
6. ad hominem
7. seed
11. argument
13. sad
14. premise
15. red herring
16. fallacy
20. ethos
21. conclusion
24. pathos
25. syllogism
26. sequitor
28. in
29. analogy
30. no
34. go
35. obit
38. my
39. ye

# 15

## Ceremonial Speaking

## CHAPTER OBJECTIVES

After reading Chapter 15, students should be able to:

1. Appreciate the importance of ceremonial speeches.

2. Identify and apply the two main techniques of ceremonial speaking: identification and magnification.

3. Define the five major types of ceremonial speeches: speeches of introduction, speeches of tribute, speeches of acceptance, speeches of inspiration, and speeches of celebration.

4. Identify the appropriate occasion for each type of ceremonial speaking.

5. Understand the role of humor in speeches of celebration.

## DISCUSSION (TEXT PP. 422–423)

**1.** The speeches in Appendix B by Bill Cosby, Elie Wiesel, and Ronald Reagan are ceremonial addresses. How do they relate to the basic questions of "Who are we?" "Why are we?" "What have we accomplished?" and "What can we become together?" What values do they celebrate? How do they achieve identification and magnification? Which tools of language do they use? Which speech designs do they follow?

**Comments:** This assignment is lengthy. You may wish to assign all or some of the questions as homework to be discussed later in class or to assign particular questions to groups for discussion in class.

As a sample answer, an evaluation of Dianne Feinstein's keynote address "Women in Politics: Time for a Change" is presented here. This speech is both persuasive and ceremonial. "Women in Politics" combines the "Who are we?" "Why are we?" and "What have we accomplished?" questions. The answer is that we (women) have altered our political perspectives since the days of Bess Truman. Feinstein argues that perhaps women have become too identified with "women's issues" and should use their unique perspective (as women) on a wider variety of issues—issues that are critical to both women and men. She recognized the accomplishments of women who have reached positions of prominence, and highlights the importance of staying power in such jobs. Feinstein both chides women for focusing too narrowly on women's issues and inspires women in all places and positions to become active by focusing their energy in one area.

The values celebrated are those of accomplishment and growth. Feinstein creates identification by mentioning such prestige sources as Margaret Thatcher, referring to the common success women have achieved, and invoking all women to bind together under a broader political agenda.

Several stylistic techniques are used, including repetition of the introductory phrases "It is time . . ." and "How can I . . . ?"

The organizational design is a combination of categorical problem-solution.

**2.** Is there a speech of inspiration you heard some time ago that you still remember? Why do you feel it made such an impression on you?

**Comments:** Many students will probably have memories of inspirational speeches, whether they were sermons, keynote addresses, or lectures by a teacher. Some of the speeches probably combined celebrational and inspirational purposes. Generally, these speeches are memorable because they touch some core value, evoke a sense of belonging, or spur us to be reinvigorated. We feel good after hearing an inspirational speech.

**3.** Do you feel you would be comfortable telling an amusing story about yourself in a speech? Why does this practice sometimes have the effect of raising a speaker's ethos?

**Comments:** While most people can use self-deprecating humor more easily than tell a joke, some students will find it easier than others. Ethos is raised by sharing personal foibles (in an appropriate speech context) because it shows the speaker has sufficient self-esteem to risk a small disclosure, and it helps create identification between the speaker and audience. To answer this question, students will probably list a number of reasons why poking fun at oneself adds to speaker ethos.

**4.** In times of death, speeches of tribute often begin a process of "mythifying" the deceased, speaking in ideal rather than real terms of the life of the person. Can this process of idealization be justified? Why or why not?

**Comments:** If students need an experience to identify with, when discussing this question, the *Challenger* disaster can serve that purpose. Speeches, poems, songs, and other forms of tribute both magnified the accomplishments of the astronauts and created identification with them for the public. The function of these speeches was to mythify the astronauts, particularly the civilian teacher on board. An examination of Reagan's *Challenger* memorial speech in Appendix B of the text will reveal some of these elements. The process is justified socially to help the survivors both heal their emotional wounds and feel that the lives of the deceased were worthwhile.

In response to this question, a variety of experiences will be related by students. Some students may recently have experienced the death of a close friend or relative. Try to focus the discussion on speeches, rather than on personal reactions: Did the eulogy magnify or mythify the person? Is mythification more likely to occur with public figures?

# APPLICATION (TEXT P. 423)

---

**1.** Prepare a speech of introduction that you might give for the next speech of one of your classmates. Which features would you select for magnification? How would you go about promoting speaker-audience identification? Would you tune the audience for the speech?

**Comments:** This exercise can be facilitated by (a) assigning each person a speaker to introduce and (b) by providing time in class for students to interview each other about their topics and themselves.

As an alternative to this assignment, have students routinely introduce classmates before they speak. This is one way of making students comfortable with the speech of introduction. Speakers will appreciate knowing someone will always be there to prepare the audience for them, and if students are trained to keep the introductions brief, the time required per speech day will be minimal.

**2.** Develop a speech of tribute in honor of a classmate, friend, or family member in which you celebrate the real and/or symbolic importance of some achievement. Remember to consider the five themes of magnification as you plan your tribute.

**Comments:** Before making this assignment, decide if you want the speeches of celebration to be primarily serious. For example, if a student reports that his greatest recent accomplishment is potty-training his child, the celebration and magnification would lend themselves to a humorous, rather than serious, treatment.

To facilitate this assignment, ask students to interview a classmate about past or recent accomplishments; then have students prepare their speeches based on the recommendations in the chapter.

**3.** Prepare a toast for a classmate whom you feel either (a) has made the most progress as a speaker this semester, or (b) who gave a speech you will likely remember long after the class is over. Strive for brevity and eloquence in your toast. Be ready to present your toast in class.

**Comments:** This can serve as a fine assignment for providing closure at the end of the semester, perhaps even at a party held on the last day of class. Some mechanism for equalizing the number of toasts given for each individual would probably help to leave all students with a positive feeling about the class (you do not want a situation where several students are not selected for toasting). Perhaps students could draw names so each would both give and receive a toast.

# ADDITIONAL EXERCISES

## TOASTING HEROES

**Purpose:** To practice the art of toasting

**Procedures:**

1. As a speech assignment, instruct students to prepare an appropriately short and eloquent toast for someone they admire (a contemporary or historic hero). Exclude class members and the instructor from receiving toasts.

2. Base your grading of the toasts on the following criteria:
(a) Appropriate demeanor when standing to give the toast
(b) Brevity
(c) Accent on the positive
(d) Memorization

(e) Focus on the hero rather than on the speaker

(f) Graphic or concrete description of accomplishment

(g) Sincerity

## MASTER OF CEREMONIES

**Purpose:** To practice the duties of a master of ceremonies

**Procedures:**

1. Throughout the semester, assign a different student to be master of ceremonies on each speech day.

2. Give the MC a list of who is speaking, one class day in advance, and discuss any timing variables or requirements of your videotape equipment.

3. On the speech day, the MC must begin the class on time, get the class's attention at the beginning of the hour, keep the speeches moving, and take care of any other demands of that day.

4. Grade the MC on how well he or she managed the entire situation while keeping the audience warmed up for the speakers.

5. Throughout the semester, discuss what makes a good MC: Do speakers feel better when they are managed by a good MC? How do speakers feel when the MC does a flippant job?

## ACCEPTANCE SPEECH ASSIGNMENT

**Purpose:** To practice preparing and presenting acceptance speeches

**Procedures:**

1. Assign a brief (3-5-minute) acceptance speech. The student should pick an award he or she hypothetically has received and prepare an acceptance speech appropriate for the occasion. Most acceptance speeches should be serious. You may wish to exclude humorous awards and humorous speeches from the assignment. Students must mention the award and presenting group during their speech.

2. Base your grading of the speech on the following criteria:

(a) Appropriateness for the group/occasion

(b) Expression of gratitude for the award

(c) Acknowledgment of those who made the accomplishment possible

(d) Focus on values inherent in the award

(e) General eloquence

# ADDITIONAL RESOURCES

"Special Speech Occasions." Films for the Humanities. 15 minutes.

Sources for tips, quotations, or stories for special speech occasions include:
*Communication Briefings* (monthly newsletter)

*Orben's Current Comedy* (biweekly magazine)

Braude, Jacob M. *Complete Speaker's and Toastmaster's Library*, 8 vols. (Englewood Cliffs, N.J.: Prentice Hall, 1965).

# Appendix A

## Group Communication

## OBSERVATIONS

Many of the exercises throughout the text require students to work in groups and apply a problem-solving process. For that reason, some instructors will prefer to cover Appendix A early in the semester. If covered at the end of the semester, students may be asked to reflect on whether or not they used the problem-solving process properly during small group work in class. If not, did it hinder their efficiency?

Students may also be asked to reflect on their participation as a group member: Did they help or hinder the group?

## ADDITIONAL RESOURCES

Cragan, John F., and David W. Wright. *Communication in Small Group Discussion: An Integrated Approach*, 2nd ed. (St. Paul, Minn.: West Publishing Co., 1980).

"How to Conduct a Meeting." Centron film (videotape). Coronet/MTI Film & Video Co. 18 minutes.

*Part IV*

# TEST QUESTIONS

# SOME NOTES ON TESTING

The purpose of testing is to assess the depth of students' understanding of the materials and skills taught. It also serves as part of a final semester grade. Many teachers prefer objective tests because they are easy to grade. Combination tests, with both objective and essay questions, sometimes provide a better assessment of students' knowledge. Questions should vary in levels of difficulty. The more difficult questions help teachers to distinguish between the good and the superior student. Tests should be constructed so that the average student can finish during the allotted time (superior students may finish in half the time; weak students may not have time to finish).

Educational literature contains much information on how to create and assess tests. See, for example: Robert L. Edel and David A. Frisbie, *Essentials of Educational Measurement*, 4th ed. (Englewood Cliffs, N.J.: Prentice-Hall, Inc. 1986). Chapters 4 and 13 of this book are particularly useful.

# CHAPTER 1: TRUE OR FALSE

Mark T if the statement is true; F if the statement is false.

_____ 1. Most of us give many informal speeches each day without realizing it.

_____ 2. Studies show oral communication skills correlate with success in employment.

_____ 3. Public speaking training can help you develop your personal sensitivity and creativity.

_____ 4. Our American political system is built on faith in communication.

_____ 5. Using accurate and objective information is a requirement of speech ethics.

_____ 6. Being careful not to persuade is a requirement of speech ethics.

_____ 7. Multisided presentations are not as successful as singlesided presentations.

_____ 8. An ethical speaker avoids unsubstantiated claims.

_____ 9. A speaker can talk about any subject without bias if careful in the approach.

_____ 10. In effect, whenever an audience listens to a speaker, its members are saying that the speaker might be a leader.

_____ 11. The speaker's success is not related to the image of the speaker held by the audience.

_____ 12. People who are competent, honest, and attractive are called ethical.

_____ 13. The message is composed only of the words you speak.

_____ 14. Radio is a medium.

_____ 15. Intelligent speech planning involves consideration of listeners.

_____ 16. Events that immediately precede your speech have no effect on the communication environment.

_____ 17. A speech may not need a clear sense of purpose to be effective.

_____ 18. The audience should be considered only after the speaker has prepared a first draft of the speech.

# CHAPTER 1: MULTIPLE-CHOICE QUESTIONS

Circle the letter of the *best* answer to each question.

1. Surveys find which of the following to be of critical importance in employment success?

    a. advanced mathematics skills

    b. listening and oral communication skills

    c. a knowledge of United States history

    d. an understanding of general social studies

    e. all of the above

2. The Oglala Sioux believed speaking well was

    a. a divine gift

    b. an inborn trait

    c. something any warrior could learn

    d. related to personal creativity

    e. all of the above

3. The benefits of public speaking training are

    a. personal

    b. social

    c. both personal and social

    d. neither personal nor social

4. The First Amendment to the Constitution prohibits laws restricting

    a. freedom of speech

    b. freedom of the press

    c. the right of peaceable assembly

    d. freedom of religion

    e. all of the above

5. Which type of speech can exert a mode of control over the audience?

    a. persuasive

    b. informative

    c. ceremonial

    d. all of the above

    e. none of the above

6. Which of the following is *not* a requirement for an ethical speech?

    a. respect for the audience

    b. no attempt to persuade the audience

    c. responsible knowledge of the topic

    d. concern for the consequences of the speech

    e. none of the above

7. An ethical speaker does which of the following?

    a. draws distinctions between fact and opinion

    b. reports the sources of factual information

    c. uses language that clarifies rather than confuses

    d. all of the above

    e. none of the above

8. Which of the following is *not* an attitude of an ethical listener?

    a. I will avoid listening to speakers with whom I disagree so I won't be per-
       suaded.

    b. Listening to those I disagree with can be most educational.

    c. I will avoid prejudging a speech topic.

    d. I will note the strengths and weaknesses of the argument.

    e. All of the above are not attitudes of an ethical listener.

9. Which of the following is *not* part of the dynamic circle?

    a. communication environment

    b. receiver

    c. medium

    d. idea

    e. All of the above are parts of the dynamic circle.

10. Which of the following is a characteristic of credibility?

   a. competence

   b. attractiveness

   c. integrity

   d. power

   e. all of the above

11. Charisma and a positive image are two components of speaker

   a. medium

   b. ideas

   c. responses

   d. ethos

   e. ethics

12. Good examples and reasons make a speech convincing by giving it

   a. substance

   b. medium

   c. communication environment

   d. ethos

   e. none of the above

13. Which of the following is a condition of the medium?

   a. the time and place when the speech is given

   b. the characteristics of the people who listen to the speech

   c. the clearness of the sound system

   d. the speaker's knowledge and vocabulary

   e. all of the above

14. Which of the following is a form of audience feedback?

   a. frowning

   b. sleeping

   c. asking questions

   d. all of the above

   e. none of the above

15. Which of the following is part of the communication environment?

    a. the topic of the speaker who precedes you

    b. the audience's expectations of what is appropriate for you to say

    c. distracting noises in the room where you speak

    d. all of the above

    e. none of the above

16. Which of the following is *not* one of the nine criteria often used to evaluate a speech?

    a. speaker commitment

    b. audience involvement

    c. substance

    d. skillful language use

    e. well-controlled environment

17. A well-chosen topic should be

    a. of interest to the speaker

    b. of interest to the audience

    c. handled within the given time limit

    d. all of the above

    e. a and b only

18. Using the pronoun *we* throughout the speech helps develop

    a. ethics

    b. audience involvement and identification

    c. substance

    d. ethical consequences

    e. speaker commitment

19. Identification is the creation of

    a. ethical consequences

    b. skillful language use

    c. speaker commitment

    d. ties between speaker, topic, and audience

    e. none of the above

20. Which of the following can be a source of substance?
    a. library research
    b. personal experiences
    c. interviews of other people
    d. all of the above
    e. none of the above

21. Adding testimony to your speech is
    a. using a clear sense of purpose
    b. using personal examples
    c. using facts and figures
    d. using the words of someone else
    e. using identification

22. The various parts of a speech are linked together by
    a. sequences
    b. credibility builders
    c. transitions
    d. translations
    e. identifications

23. Skillful language use means using
    a. long, complex sentences
    b. abstract words
    c. chains of dependent clauses
    d. concrete words
    e. all of the above

24. The type of speech presentation most often recommended in speech classes is
    a. impromptu
    b. extemporaneous
    c. memorized
    d. written out
    e. translated

# CHAPTER 1: SHORT-ANSWER QUESTIONS

Put the correct answer in each blank.

1. Freedom of speech is protected by the _____ to the Constitution of the United States.

2. The communication process can be visualized as a _____ because of the ever-changing relationships among its parts.

3. Communication begins with a _____, the person who initiates the speech.

4. The message travels through some _____, usually the air.

5. The listener who processes the message is called the _____.

6. The speech occurs within a communication _____, which can help or impede the process.

7. _____ was one of the first people to identify the components of credibility.

# CHAPTER 1: ESSAY QUESTIONS

Answer each question in detail.

1. Draw, label, and explain the parts of the dynamic circle of the communication process.

2. Contrast the ethical responsibilities of the speaker and the listener.

3. List and discuss four of the nine criteria used to evaluate a public speech.

4. Describe a speaker who you believe has high ethos. Identify the characteristics that make this person credible to you.

5. List and explain three personal benefits of public speaking training.

# CHAPTER 2: TRUE-FALSE QUESTIONS

Mark T if the statement if true; F if the statement is false.

_____ 1. Most of us underestimate our own speaking ability.

_____ 2. Most of the abilities that define leadership are inborn.

_____ 3. The greater the power of a speaker to affect the reception of a message, the more likely that listeners will respond to that speaker as a leader.

_____ 4. A well-organized speech adds to the audience's perceptions of speaker competence.

_____ 5. A speaker who conveys power appears honest and dependable.

_____ 6. Conferred power is derived from your manner and nonverbal communication.

_____ 7. It is more important for you to appear confident than to feel confident.

_____ 8. In an introductory speech, you want to tell your whole life story.

_____ 9. Your introductory speech establishes your credibility for future speeches.

_____ 10. Because the introductory speech is short, its design must be complex.

_____ 11. Different topics or purposes suggest different principles of design.

_____ 12. As separate parts of the speech, the introduction, body, and conclusion need not fit together coherently.

_____ 13. Startling the audience in the introduction is an inappropriate technique.

_____ 14. The central idea of a speech is called the introduction.

_____ 15. It is a bad idea to refer to previous speakers in your introduction.

_____ 16. A short speech should include many different points.

_____ 17. Narrative examples should use abstract language.

# CHAPTER 2: MULTIPLE-CHOICE QUESTIONS

Circle the letter of the *best* answer to each question.

1. The introductory speeches of your classmates can

    a. provide useful insights into the nature of your listeners

    b. prove helpful to you in preparing later speeches

    c. help you select topics for your later speeches

    d. help break the ice between you and your classmates

    e. all of the above

2. Competence is

    a. an inborn characteristic

    b. based on your knowledge, education, and experience

    c. the same as ethos

    d. another term for empathy

    e. none of the above

3. Competence can be enhanced by

    a. selecting topics you already know something about

    b. doing research to qualify yourself to speak responsibly

    c. citing authoritative sources

    d. using personal experiences to add authenticity

    e. all of the above

4. Audiences form impressions of speakers based on the speakers'

    a. attractiveness

    b. power

    c. competence

    d. integrity

    e. all of the above

5. Integrity is enhanced when you
    a. select a topic requiring no research or preparation
    b. read your speech word for word to use precise language
    c. show different sides of an issue and explain why you have chosen your position
    d. ask your listeners to commit to an attitude, even if you cannot
    e. none of the above

6. Identification is
    a. extreme ethics
    b. a feeling of closeness between speaker and listener
    c. an image of power and control
    d. assigned responsibility and status
    e. unimportant in speeches

7. Identification can be achieved by
    a. sharing feelings as well as thoughts
    b. using natural gestures
    c. sharing stories that listeners can relate to
    d. all of the above
    e. none of the above

8. Assigned power is
    a. natural
    b. neutral
    c. conferred
    d. credible
    e. conscientious

9. The controlling idea of a speech determines the
    a. environment of the speech
    b. chronological design
    c. principle of design
    d. spatial design
    e. none of the above

10. Which of the following would use a categorical design? A description of
    a. the steps in developing good photographs
    b. how a special person changed your life
    c. the effects of sports—teammates, competition, physical challenge—on your life
    d. all of the above
    e. none of the above

11. Which of the following is *not* a basic purpose of the introduction?
    a. to relate important facts about your subject
    b. to arouse audience interest
    c. to prepare the audience for the rest of your speech
    d. All of the above are basic purposes.
    e. None of the above are basic purposes.

12. The main points of a speech are developed in the
    a. introduction
    b. thematic statement
    c. body
    d. conclusion
    e. spatial design

13. Extended stories used for illustration are called
    a. introductions
    b. thematic statements
    c. principles of design
    d. narratives
    e. transitions

14. Narratives should
    a. be short and to the point
    b. develop a feeling of closeness between the speaker and the audience
    c. hold the interest of the audience
    d. reveal some truth about the speaker or topic
    e. all of the above

15. In using a narrative to illustrate a point, the speaker should
    a. use colorful language
    b. use concrete words
    c. use active tenses
    d. have a lively, interesting presentation style
    e. all of the above

16. The introductory speech should be presented
    a. after memorizing it word for word
    b. by reading from the preparation outline
    c. in an impromptu manner
    d. by reading from a manuscript
    e. none of the above

17. The ideal presentation sounds like
    a. improved conversation
    b. dramatic conversation
    c. insipid conversation
    d. inspired conversation
    e. inspirational conversation

18. The habit of replacing negative thought patterns with their positive counterparts is called
    a. performance anxiety
    b. narrative structuring
    c. cognitive restructuring
    d. extemporaneous structuring
    e. improved conversation

# CHAPTER 2: SHORT-ANSWER QUESTIONS

Put the correct answer in each blank.

1. A speaker who conveys _____, a dimension of ethos, appears honest and dependable.

2. _____ power is derived from assigned responsibilities and status.

3. The central idea of a speech is expressed in the _____ statement.

4. A condensed version of the preparation outline is called the _____ outline.

5. Replacing negative thought patterns with positive ones is called _____ _____.

6. Signs of _____, like wearing similar clothing, create links between the speaker and the audience.

7. The type of presentation recommended by the authors is _____.

# CHAPTER 2: ESSAY QUESTIONS

Answer each question in detail.

1. List and discuss three specific recommendations for handling performance anxiety.

2. Explain three specific things you can do to increase your credibility with the class.

3. Differentiate between conferred and natural power. Do you have either kind of power in this class?

4. Write a narrative describing an experience you have had.

5. You have been invited to speak to the local chamber of commerce at a business luncheon. Many community leaders are members of the chamber. Discuss two steps you could take to create identification with this audience.

# CHAPTER 3: TRUE-FALSE QUESTIONS

Mark T if the statement is true; F if the statement is false.

_____ 1. There can be no communication without listening.

_____ 2. If listening does not work well, the dynamic circle of communication is broken.

_____ 3. Leaders need not be good listeners.

_____ 4. Listening is an automatic, physiological process.

_____ 5. A critical listener attends to all stimuli in the environment.

_____ 6. A critical listener extracts value from a message.

_____ 7. Effective listeners ask questions to harass speakers.

_____ 8. Critical listeners listen creatively.

_____ 9. A survey of Fortune 500 companies found that poor listening is related to low productivity.

_____ 10. Many leading companies in the United States have invested heavily in listening training for employees.

_____ 11. Critical listening ability can be learned.

_____ 12. Disorganized speech content makes it difficult to listen well.

_____ 13. The usual public speaking rate is about 125 words per minute.

_____ 14. The usual rate of processing information is about 100 words per minute.

_____ 15. Personal dislike of a speaker can be a common cause of listener problems.

_____ 16. People tend to listen less critically to speeches that support their own position.

_____ 17. The speaker is the person most responsible for effective communication.

_____ 18. Effective listeners pay attention only to words.

# CHAPTER 3: MULTIPLE-CHOICE QUESTIONS

Circle the letter of the *best* answer to each question.

1. Adults spend _____ percent of their communication time listening.
   a. 10 to 20
   b. 20 to 30
   c. 30 to 40
   d. 40 to 50
   e. 50 to 60

2. Adults retain about _____ percent of what they hear.
   a. 20 to 25
   b. 30 to 35
   c. 40 to 45
   d. 50 to 55
   e. 60 to 65

3. Attending, comprehending, and interpreting are components of
   a. hearing
   b. speaking
   c. critical listening
   d. all of the above
   e. none of the above

4. Which of the following is *not* a characteristic of critical listening?
   a. paying attention
   b. hearing
   c. interpreting
   d. remembering
   e. All of the above are characteristics of critical thinking.

5. Critical listening skills are helpful
   a. with friends
   b. in the classroom
   c. at work
   d. all of the above
   e. none of the above

6. Fortune 500 companies report that listening skills
   a. are not important in hiring new employees
   b. are not related to job performance
   c. are useful for managers but not lower-ranking employees
   d. are related to productivity
   e. all of the above

7. Critical listening can
   a. help improve job performance
   b. increase one's personal credibility
   c. help you distinguish between ethical and unethical advertisements
   d. all of the above
   e. none of the above

8. Listening problems can be caused by
   a. a speaker's negative ethos
   b. fuzzy ideas
   c. noises in the environment
   d. a receiver's attitudes
   e. all of the above

9. Which of the following is a good reason not to listen?
   a. The source speaks in a monotone.
   b. The speaker seems incompetent.
   c. The speech is disorganized.
   d. all of the above
   e. none of the above

10. Which of the following can be an environmental distraction to listening?

    a. detailed charts or graphs

    b. denotative meanings of words

    c. connotative meanings of words

    d. an eloquent presentation

    e. bad listening habits

11. Speakers usually speak about _____ words per minute.

    a. 50

    b. 125

    c. 200

    d. 275

    e. 350

12. Listeners can process information at about _____ words per minute.

    a. 100

    b. 125

    c. 150

    d. 200

    e. 500

13. The denotative meaning of a word is

    a. its dictionary definition

    b. the feelings it arouses in you

    c. its associational meaning

    d. related to how fast it is processed by listeners

    e. a reason to stop listening

14. A connotative meaning of the word *dog* might be

    a. a canine animal

    b. a four-legged animal

    c. a four-legged, domesticated animal

    d. a friendly, devoted animal

    e. none of the above

# CHAPTER 4: TRUE-FALSE QUESTIONS

Mark T if the statement is true; F if the statement is false.

_____ 1. A good speech topic must be about an earth-shaking issue.

_____ 2. To select a good speech topic, you must know something about your listeners.

_____ 3. The best way to begin your topic search is to check the amount of preparation it will entail.

_____ 4. A good rule of topic selection is to match your personal interests with those of the audience.

_____ 5. You can find speech topics in magazines.

_____ 6. You can create a good speech by summarizing magazine articles.

_____ 7. The *Who, What, When* . . . method of topic analysis works only for informative topics.

_____ 8. To persuade may be the general purpose of a speech.

_____ 9. To celebrate may be the specific purpose of a speech.

_____ 10. The specific purpose of your speech is usually assigned by the instructor.

_____ 11. The thematic statement is always stated in the beginning section of your speech.

_____ 12. Atlases are useless in preparing speeches because they only contain maps.

_____ 13. It is never wise to use personal information in a speech.

_____ 14. The card catalog can help you find a listing of magazine articles about your topic.

_____ 15. Encyclopedias are the most useful places to find all the current, timely information you need for a speech.

_____ 16. To find detailed and specialized articles about your topic, you should consult an index to periodicals.

_____ 17. Most libraries do not contain atlases.

_____ 18. Many libraries maintain a vertical file on topics of local interest.

# CHAPTER 4: MULTIPLE-CHOICE QUESTIONS

Circle the letter of the *best* answer to each question.

1. A good speech topic is
   a. about an earth-shaking issue
   b. important to you personally
   c. appropriate to any conceivable audience
   d. all of the above
   e. none of the above

2. A good speech topic is appropriate to the
   a. audience
   b. context
   c. time
   d. purpose of the occasion
   e. all of the above

3. When selecting a topic, it is important to
   a. expand it to include all possible elements
   b. prepare twice as much material as your time limit permits
   c. narrow the subject to some aspect important to your audience
   d. all of the above
   e. none of the above

4. Which of the following is an appropriately narrowed topic?
   a. nuclear waste
   b. nuclear war
   c. antinuclear activism in your community
   d. the peace movement
   e. all of the above

5. Which of the following is a stage in the topic discovery process?

   a. charting your own interests and the audience's interests

   b. focusing and analyzing potential topics

   c. identifying shared interests

   d. all of the above

   e. none of the above

6. Asking "Why do I want to give a speech on this topic?" helps determine your

   a. prestige

   b. identification

   c. research base

   d. thesis

   e. purpose

7. Which of the following is a general speech purpose?

   a. to persuade

   b. to entertain

   c. to celebrate

   d. all of the above

   e. none of the above

8. Which of the following is a specific purpose?

   a. to entertain the audience

   b. to explain how horses are trained

   c. to inform the audience about horses

   d. to persuade the audience

   e. none of the above

9. After determining the specific purpose, you should consider

   a. if the specific purpose has something new to offer your audience

   b. if the specific purpose is important enough to deserve close attention

   c. if the specific purpose is too ambitious for the allotted time

   d. all of the above

   e. none of the above

10. The central idea of your message is the
    a. general purpose
    b. specific purpose
    c. thematic statement
    d. transition
    e. topic

11. Which of the following is *not* one of the basic sources of information available to speakers?
    a. personal experience
    b. library
    c. interviews
    d. All of the above are basic sources.
    e. None of the above are basic sources.

12. Personal experience
    a. can add credibility and authenticity to a speech
    b. should never be used as the sole source of information
    c. can be arranged as part of the research for a speech
    d. all of the above
    e. none of the above

13. The goal of researching your topic is to obtain
    a. the general purpose of your speech
    b. impressive statistics
    c. the specific purpose of your speech
    d. responsible knowledge of your topic
    e. all of the above

14. To find the most recent article published on your topic, you should first consult the library's
    a. card catalog
    b. reference room
    c. government documents section
    d. special collections area
    e. holding area

15. Which of the following are *not* usually found in the reference room?

    a. indexes

    b. abstracts

    c. sources of timely facts

    d. encyclopedias

    e. government documents

16. Which of the following is *not* a source of timely facts?

    a. an encyclopedia

    b. a newspaper index

    c. *Facts on File*

    d. *Congressional Quarterly*

    e. All of the above are sources of timely facts.

17. You should prepare for an interview by

    a. writing a letter in advance to the person you wish to interview

    b. planning your major questions

    c. learning about the topic in advance

    d. all of the above

    e. none of the above

18. When should controversial questions be asked in an interview?

    a. at the beginning

    b. in the middle

    c. toward the end

    d. in advance, in writing

    e. never

19. "Could you tell me more about . . . ?" is which type of question?

    a. mirror

    b. verifier

    c. reinforcer

    d. probe

    e. none of the above

20. Information should be tested for
   a. reliability
   b. timeliness
   c. precision
   d. thoroughness
   e. all of the above

# CHAPTER 4: SHORT-ANSWER QUESTIONS

Put the correct answer in each blank.

1. Asking "Why do I want to give a speech on this topic?" helps determine your over-all _____ _____.

2. Entertaining, persuading, and informing are _____ purposes of a speech.

3. The _____ purpose of a speech states exactly what you wish to accomplish.

4. The central idea of your speech is articulated in the _____ _____.

5. Interview questions that reflect back part of a response are called _____ _____.

# CHAPTER 4: ESSAY QUESTIONS

Answer each question in detail.

1. Name Rudyard Kipling's "six honest serving-men" and describe how they are helpful in analyzing a possible topic area.

2. You have been invited to speak to a group of high-school students about the social side of college. State both a specific purpose and a general purpose for this topic (and audience).

3. You have decided to give a speech on the effects of radon in homes. Using the advice in Chapter 4, state where you would first seek information in the library. Then state three specific sources you would consult for which types of information.

4. Discuss three criteria for testing information.

5. Explain two types of questions used in interviews, giving an example of each.

# CHAPTER 5: TRUE-FALSE QUESTIONS

Mark T if the statement is true; F if the statement is false.

_____ 1. The target audience is that group capable of making the speaker's words effective.

_____ 2. The time of day of the presentation is an important factor in adapting to the occasion.

_____ 3. Speaking louder is the only way to adapt to noisy environments.

_____ 4. The atmosphere or mood created by previous speakers is the stereotyping effect.

_____ 5. Audiences have definite ideas about what is and is not appropriate for specific speech occasions.

_____ 6. The size of your audience makes little difference when planning your speech.

_____ 7. With larger audiences you should speak slower and louder.

_____ 8. Audience analysis deals only with absolute information about the listeners.

_____ 9. Older listeners are more easily persuaded than younger listeners.

_____ 10. According to a *USA Today* survey, college students are optimistic about the future.

_____ 11. Sex is as good a predictor of audience behavior today as it was 20 years ago.

_____ 12. Females are much more easily persuaded than males.

_____ 13. Education is generally a better indicator of listeners' interests than is their age or sex.

_____ 14. Better-educated audiences know more, and so are usually more prejudiced and dogmatic.

_____ 15. Surveys show that more highly educated groups are not as worried about financial security as less well-educated groups.

_____ 16. Everyone in an occupational group will hold the same opinion.

_____ 17. Members of the Audubon Society belong to the same occupational group.

_____ 18. Values concerned with how we should behave are called instrumental values.

_____ 19. The co-active approach recommends the use of threats to persuade an audience.

# CHAPTER 5: MULTIPLE-CHOICE QUESTIONS

Circle the letter of the *best* answer to each question.

1. Which of the following is a factor in analyzing the speech occasion?
   a. why the audience attended
   b. demographic characteristics of the audience
   c. sexual stereotyping of the audience
   d. religious preferences of listeners
   e. all of the above

2. On the morning of your speech on nuclear disarmament, you read that a civil defense drill on how to respond during a nuclear war is taking place next week. You should
   a. ignore the new information since you've already written your speech
   b. drop your prepared speech and speak extemporaneously about the drill
   c. call in sick so you will have time to rewrite your speech
   d. refer to the drill early in your speech
   e. drop one main point and replace it with a section on the drill

3. The larger your audience is,
   a. the more jokes you should use
   b. the more formal you should be
   c. the more you should try to have eye contact with everyone
   d. the more informal you should be
   e. none of the above

4. With a larger audience, you should
   a. speak louder
   b. enunciate more clearly
   c. speak slower
   d. all of the above
   e. none of the above

5. Which of the following is *not* demographic information?

   a. age

   b. sex

   c. occasion

   d. educational level

   e. sociocultural background

6. Assuming men are more interested in hope repair than women is an example of

   a. sexual stereotyping

   b. sexist language

   c. demographic analysis

   d. preliminary tuning

   e. none of the above

7. Saying that all the girls on the cheerleading squad are dumb blondes is

   a. sexual stereotyping

   b. using sexist-language trigger words

   c. using archetypal images

   d. both a and b

   e. none of the above

8. The more educated your audience is,

   a. the more they know about general topics

   b. the broader their range of interests is

   c. the more critically they listen

   d. the less prejudiced they are

   e. all of the above

9. With a highly educated audience, you should

   a. acknowledge opposing viewpoints during your speech

   b. ignore opposing viewpoints and press your own view

   c. use more trigger words

   d. be more dogmatic

   e. all of the above

10. Which of the following uses an archetypal image?
    a. We don't need more dumb jocks on this campus.
    b. The human race can move forward and reach the stars if only we keep trying.
    c. AIDS may be only a small tropical storm right now, but it's gathering hurricane force.
    d. Can the door to your home be opened with a credit card?
    e. both b and c

11. Motivations, attitudes, and values are
    a. demographic factors
    b. audience dynamics factors
    c. occasion factors
    d. preliminary tuning factors
    e. archetypal images

12. Motivational factors are
    a. relevant to both persuasive and informative speeches
    b. useful in arousing the interest of the audience
    c. shared by all human beings
    d. all of the above
    e. none of the above

13. Which of the following are *not* included in Maslow's hierarchy of needs?
    a. physiological needs
    b. safety needs
    c. dominance needs
    d. esteem needs
    e. self-actualization needs

14. A debate-team recruitment speech that stresses the joy of winning trophies and recognition is appealing to
    a. physiological needs
    b. safety needs
    c. belongingness needs
    d. esteem needs
    e. self-actualization needs

15. A debate-team recruitment speech that stresses the joy of beating the other team in head-to-head competition is appealing to

    a. physiological needs

    b. dominance needs

    c. self-actualization needs

    d. belongingness needs

    e. safety needs

16. Internal mental responses that locate ideas on a scale of judgment are

    a. needs for change

    b. behaviors

    c. values

    d. attitudes

    e. none of the above

17. Which of the following is *not* a step in the co-active approach?

    a. establish identification between speaker and listeners

    b. avoid the use of threats

    c. use strong emotional appeals and archetypal images

    d. limit what you hope to accomplish

    e. provide information on opposing positions

18. Which of the following is a terminal value identified by Rokeach?

    a. ambition

    b. a comfortable life

    c. dominance

    d. responsibility

    e. honesty

19. Which of the following is an instrumental value identified by Rokeach?

    a. a comfortable life

    b. world peace

    c. honesty

    d. freedom

    e. none of the above

20. When the Studies Abroad office argues that you should spend a term overseas to break up the routine of college, it is appealing to your
    a. belongingness needs
    b. self-actualization needs
    c. need for independence
    d. need for change
    e. none of the above

# CHAPTER 5: SHORT-ANSWER QUESTIONS

Put the correct answer in each blank.

1. Anything that has happened in the immediate past becomes part of the _____ of your speech.

2. The atmosphere or mood created by previous speeches is called the _____ _____ effect.

3. Objective characteristics of the audience are _____ data.

4. Making overly broad generalizations about members of a group is called _____.

5. Consistently using the word *she* to refer to *nurses* is an example of _____ language.

6. Metaphors based on experiences common to all people are _____.

# CHAPTER 5: ESSAY QUESTIONS

Answer each question in detail.

1. You have planned a speech on the rising cost of liability insurance. On the morning of your speech, you learn in the newspaper that liability reform is being discussed in the legislature. Discuss the advantages and disadvantages of slightly altering your speech to include this information.

2. Explain two ways you can discover demographic information about an audience.

3. Discuss why a speaker must understand the concepts of human motivation and how that knowledge should be used in developing a speech.

4. A demographic analysis shows that your audience for a speech on AIDS is middle-aged, male members of the Retail Food Manufacturers Association. Discuss what inferences about the audience you can draw and how these inferences can help you shape your speech.

5. Explain how a speaker can determine the needs, or motivations, important to an audience.

# CHAPTER 6: TRUE-FALSE QUESTIONS

Mark T if the statement is true; F if the statement is false.

_____ 1. Disorganized messages negatively affect the way the speaker is perceived.

_____ 2. Simple designs are preferable to elaborate designs in public speaking.

_____ 3. In general, the fewer main points you have, the better.

_____ 4. Parallelism both simplifies main points and makes them more memorable.

_____ 5. Proper balance among the parts of a speech is called simplicity.

_____ 6. If you follow the principle of progression, each main point receives equal treatment.

_____ 7. The introduction and the conclusion should be approximately the same length.

_____ 8. When you balance the amount of time spent on each main point, you are using the quality of speech coherence.

_____ 9. It is wise to limit yourself to no more than three main points in a short speech.

_____ 10. Undeveloped main points damage your credibility.

_____ 11. Categorical designs order events sequentially.

_____ 12. Problem-solution and cause-effect designs are often used together.

_____ 13. Supporting materials provide the substance of a speech.

_____ 14. There is a precise equation to determine how much supporting material is needed.

_____ 15. The greater the risk for your listeners, the less you must reassure them with supporting material.

_____ 16. The further a subject may seem from the everyday lives of your listeners, the more examples you should use.

_____ 17. Transitions signal the listener that the speaker is leaving one point and going on to another.

_____ 18. A preview leaves the audience with a sense of closure about a speech.

# CHAPTER 6: MULTIPLE-CHOICE QUESTIONS

Circle the letter of the *best* answer to each question.

1. The principle of good form is explained by the principles of
   a. closure
   b. proximity
   c. Gehring psychology
   d. Gestalt psychology
   e. none of the above

2. Which of the following is a quality of good form?
   a. simplicity
   b. sympathy
   c. synchronicity
   d. imbalance
   e. thematic statements

3. Speech structure may be simplified by
   a. reducing the number of main points
   b. using simple, direct language to phrase main points
   c. using parallel phrasing for main points
   d. all of the above
   e. none of the above

4. Which of the following is important to symmetry?
   a. having an introduction the same size as the body
   b. having a conclusion the same size as the body
   c. having a body longer than the introduction or conclusion
   d. all of the above
   e. none of the above

5. The longest part of a speech should be the
   a. introduction
   b. thematic statement
   c. body
   d. conclusion
   e. transitions

6. Relating the parts of a speech to each other makes the speech
   a. timely
   b. coherent
   c. equitable
   d. progressive
   e. thematic

7. One of the three main tasks of structuring the body of a speech is
   a. determining the thematic statement
   b. deciding how to support the main points
   c. deciding on the introduction
   d. preparing the conclusion
   e. all of the above

8. A main point must be grounded firmly by
   a. the thematic statement
   b. the introduction
   c. supporting materials
   d. the conclusion
   e. all of the above

9. In a longer speech, it is wise to limit yourself to no more than _____ main points.
   a. two
   b. three
   c. five
   d. seven
   e. eight

10. According to the principle of proximity,
    a. things that occur together in time and space should be discussed in that manner
    b. things that are similar in some way should be discussed together
    c. things should be tied together with transitions
    d. things should be neatly tied together by the conclusion
    e. the introduction should be near the body

11. To describe a process involving three steps, you should use a
    a. problem-solution pattern
    b. sequential pattern
    c. spatial pattern
    d. categorical pattern
    e. none of the above

12. In a speech about places you visited on a cross-country drive, you should use a
    a. problem-solution design
    b. cause-effect design
    c. spatial design
    d. categorical design
    e. none of the above

13. When a story is incomplete, your annoyance relates to a violation of
    a. the principle of categorization
    b. the principle of proximity
    c. the principle of similarity
    d. the principle of closure
    e. the principle of cause-effect

14. Supporting materials include
    a. statistics
    b. lay opinions
    c. stories
    d. all of the above
    e. none of the above

15. The less credible you are on an issue,

   a. the more stories you should use

   b. the more objective supporting material you should use

   c. the more comparisons you should use

   d. the less examples you should use

   e. the less human interest you should use

16. The ideal model for supporting a main point includes

   a. the most important relevant hard data

   b. the most authoritative judgments by reputable sources

   c. at least one graphic story or example or narrative

   d. all of the above

   e. none of the above

17. The introduction of your speech can arouse listeners' interest by

   a. establishing your credibility as a speaker

   b. stating the thematic statement

   c. beginning with a quotation

   d. all of the above

   e. none of the above

18. One purpose of the conclusion is to

   a. establish your credibility

   b. provide closure

   c. arouse interest in your topic

   d. all of the above

   e. none of the above

19. The elements that link the parts of your speech together are

   a. identifications

   b. closures

   c. quotations

   d. conclusions

   e. transitions

# CHAPTER 6: SHORT-ANSWER QUESTIONS

Put the correct answer in each blank.

1. Proper balance among the parts of a speech represents the principle of _____.

2. A transition that reminds the audience of points you have made in one portion of your speech is a(n) _____ _____.

3. A transition between the introduction and the body of a speech that tells listeners what you are going to tell them is a(n) _____.

4. Arranging your main points in chronological order uses a(n) _____ pattern.

5. Questions used to arouse attention, rather than seek information, are _____ questions.

6. Telling the entire story delivers a sense of completeness, or _____.

7. Arranging your main points by their physical relationships uses a(n) _____ pattern of organization.

# CHAPTER 6: ESSAY QUESTIONS

Answer each question in detail.

1. Discuss two ways to arouse interest in the introduction of a speech.

2. Describe two techniques for concluding a speech.

3. Write an introduction for a speech on class registration, using a rhetorical question.

4. Describe two types of supporting materials. Discuss their usefulness.

5. Prepare an effective conclusion to a speech on overcoming performance anxiety. Use one of the techniques described in Chapter 6.

# CHAPTER 7: TRUE-FALSE QUESTIONS

Mark T if the statement is true; F if the statement is false.

_____ 1. An outline helps you determine if you have enough supporting materials.

_____ 2. The preparation outline is tentative and may undergo many changes.

_____ 3. The preparation outline contains the three main parts of a speech.

_____ 4. A speech may have sub-subpoints.

_____ 5. Never overestimate your audience's information.

_____ 6. Never underestimate your audience's intelligence.

_____ 7. A speech may go through several preparation outlines before you find the right approach.

_____ 8. Preparation outlines strictly adhere to rules of coordination.

_____ 9. Classroom speeches may not require titles.

_____ 10. A title should promise everything to an audience, regardless of the speaker's ability to deliver.

_____ 11. Statements at the same outline level should receive about the same degree of support.

_____ 12. You should use the same type of supporting material under each point to fulfill the principle of coordination.

_____ 13. Statements on an outline should be indented to show their relative subordination.

_____ 14. Main points should be worded as complex sentences.

_____ 15. Formal outlines should be used as notes as you present your speech.

_____ 16. In reference citations, titles precede authors' names.

# CHAPTER 7: MULTIPLE-CHOICE QUESTIONS

Circle the letter of the *best* answer to each question.

1. You may prepare how many different types of outlines when planning a speech?
   a. only one
   b. only two
   c. as many as three
   d. as many as four
   e. as many as five

2. The tentative, changeable outline is called the
   a. formal outline
   b. key-word outline
   c. preparation outline
   d. all of the above
   e. none of the above

3. In addition to your main points, your preparation outline should contain your
   a. topic
   b. specific purpose
   c. thematic statement
   d. all of the above
   e. none of the above

4. The foundation of your outline is
   a. the specific purpose, topic, and thematic statement
   b. the introduction, body, and conclusion
   c. the preview, transitions, and subpoints
   d. the key-word, formal, and preparation outlines
   e. none of the above

5. Subpoints are
   a. thematic statements
   b. the purpose of the speech
   c. the transitions
   d. the divisions of a main point
   e. all of the above

6. If your preparation outline seems too ambitious for the audience and time limit, you should
   a. get a new topic
   b. get a new audience
   c. deliver the speech anyway
   d. narrow your topic
   e. eliminate two main points

7. A formal outline and preparation outline are different because
   a. the formal outline must have a title
   b. the formal outline has a clear separation between the introduction, body, and conclusion
   c. the formal outline strictly adheres to rules of coordination and subordination
   d. none of the above
   e. all of the above

8. A formal outline includes
   a. a clear separation of foundation and superstructure
   b. strict adherence to the rules of coordination
   c. main points as simple, independent sentences
   d. all of the above
   e. none of the above

9. Titles can do all of the following *except*
   a. arouse curiosity
   b. express the theme
   c. act as supporting material
   d. repeat the central message throughout the speech
   e. prepare the audience for the speech

10. The principle of coordination states that
    a.  points of equal importance should be on the same outline level
    b.  points on the same outline level should receive the same support
    c.  equal points need not be supported by the same category of support
    d.  all of the above
    e.  none of the above

11. According to the principle of subordination, main points are
    a.  more specific than those that follow
    b.  more general than those that follow
    c.  supporting material for the points that follow
    d.  the same as subpoints
    e.  the same as sub-subpoints

12. Main points should be worded in formal outlines as
    a.  abstract language
    b.  formal, complex sentences
    c.  multiclause sentences
    d.  simple, independent clauses or sentences
    e.  all of the above

13. Parallel construction means
    a.  the main points have the same importance as the subpoints
    b.  only even numbers of main points are allowed
    c.  the same type of phrase or clause introduces each main point
    d.  only odd numbers of main points are allowed
    e.  none of the above

14. Controversial main points should
    a.  be avoided
    b.  be offered without supporting materials
    c.  be offered with supporting materials
    d.  use only facts as support
    e.  use only testimony as support

15. The type of outline used during the presentation of a speech is a
    a. preparation outline
    b. key-word outline
    c. formal outline
    d. any of the above
    e. none of the above

16. The key-word outline is
    a. written out word for word
    b. written in complete sentences
    c. never more than one index card long
    d. shorter than the preparation or formal outline
    e. all of the above

17. Facts, testimony, and examples are
    a. main points
    b. subpoints
    c. supporting materials
    d. principles of coordination
    e. principles of subordination

18. In reference citations for books, the city of publication
    a. precedes the author's name
    b. precedes the title of the work
    c. precedes the publisher
    d. follows the date
    e. follows the page number

19. If you cannot find any supporting material for a main point,
    a. it must be self-evident
    b. it probably does not deserve attention
    c. you should move it earlier in the outline
    d. you should move it later in the outline
    e. none of the above

# CHAPTER 7: SHORT-ANSWER QUESTIONS

Put the correct answer in each blank.

1. The major divisions of a main point are called _____.

2. The principle of _____ requires that statements of equal importance be placed on the same level of the outline.

3. The principle of _____ requires that statements descend in importance from Roman numerals to capital letters to arabic numbers, and so forth.

4. Using the same phrase to begin each main point is _____ construction.

5. During the presentation of your speech, you should use a(n) _____ outline.

6. The first outline you create is called the _____ outline.

# CHAPTER 7: ESSAY QUESTIONS

Answer each question in detail.

1. Name and differentiate between the three types of outlines.

2. Explain the principle of coordination.

3. Explain the principle of subordination.

4. Write three main points in parallel construction and explain why parallel construction is advantageous.

# CHAPTER 8: TRUE-FALSE QUESTIONS

Mark T if the statement is true; F if the statement is false.

_____ 1. Sometimes visual aids are superior to words in conveying meaning.

_____ 2. Using visual aids increases speech anxiety.

_____ 3. There are only four kinds of visual aids.

_____ 4. The speaker is the first visual aid your audience is exposed to.

_____ 5. When using classmates as visual aids in your speech, it is best to ask for spontaneous volunteers during the speech.

_____ 6. If a visual aid is too small, it hurts more than it helps.

_____ 7. Commercially prepared maps are perfect visual aids.

_____ 8. Labeling the lines on a graph is the best way to clarify which line is which.

_____ 9. A pictograph is an image symbolizing the information it represents.

_____ 10. A photograph is always worth a thousand words in public speaking.

_____ 11. Darkening the room is a disadvantage of using slides.

_____ 12. A videotape is a good visual aid for a short speech.

_____ 13. The chalkboard is useful for spontaneous drawings.

_____ 14. You should try not to turn your back on your listeners.

_____ 15. Handouts are a high risk way to present visual aids.

_____ 16. Color can be used to reinforce impressions.

# CHAPTER 8: MULTIPLE-CHOICE QUESTIONS

Circle the letter of the *best* answer to each question.

1. Visual aids are helpful as a means of
    a. additional sensory contact for the audience
    b. overcoming the abstractness of words
    c. overcoming the inherent weaknesses of words
    d. all of the above
    e. none of the above

2. Which of the following is *not* a good use for visual aids?
    a. to fill time in a speech
    b. to enhance understanding
    c. to add authenticity
    d. to add variety
    e. to help the message have lasting impact

3. The easiest way to illustrate a proper golf swing is to use which of the following visual aids?
    a. the speaker
    b. a sketch
    c. a map
    d. a graph
    e. a chart

4. Models are useful when the actual subject is
    a. too small
    b. too big
    c. too expensive
    d. all of the above
    e. none of the above

5. A well-designed graph is particularly useful to present
    a. expert testimony
    b. lay testimony
    c. statistics
    d. examples
    e. analogies

6. Who reports to whom in an organization could best be shown by a
    a. sequence chart
    b. pie graph
    c. line graph
    d. flow chart
    e. stream chart

7. An aid that shows successive parts of a process on different poster boards is a
    a. sequence chart
    b. pie graph
    c. line graph
    d. flow chart
    e. stream chart

8. Photographs are *not* useful when they
    a. contain too much detail
    b. are too small
    c. are circulated among the audience
    d. all of the above
    e. none of the above

9. Disadvantages of the chalkboard include
    a. sloppy drawings
    b. sacrifice of eye contact with audience
    c. overuse as a visual aid
    d. all of the above
    e. none of the above

10. You should write on flip charts with

    a. chalk

    b. pencils

    c. pens

    d. broad felt markers

    e. paint

11. Which of the following is *not* a principle of visual aid design?

    a. The visual aid should emphasize what the speech emphasizes.

    b. The visual aid should seem balanced and pleasing to the eye.

    c. The visual aid should be easy for the audience to see.

    d. The visual aid should be beautiful.

    e. The visual aid should be easy for you to use.

12. A visual aid should have

    a. lots of white space

    b. balance in how words or pictures are spaced

    c. an uncrowded look

    d. all of the above

    e. none of the above

13. Color can

    a. add impact to visual aids

    b. convey or enhance meaning

    c. reinforce moods

    d. all of the above

    e. none of the above

14. Which type of color scheme shows the similarity of concepts?

    a. analogous

    b. supplementary

    c. complementary

    d. both a and b

    e. both b and c

15. Which of the following is a guideline for visual aid usage?
    a. plan
    b. practice
    c. Don't display aids until you are ready to use them.
    d. all of the above
    e. none of the above

# CHAPTER 8: SHORT-ANSWER QUESTIONS

Put the correct answer in each blank.

1. A _____ color scheme uses variations of one color.

2. _____ colors are adjacent on a color wheel.

3. _____ colors are opposite on the color wheel.

4. _____ graphs are circular in form.

5. _____ graphs are best to show trends over time.

# CHAPTER 8: ESSAY QUESTIONS

Answer each question in detail.

1. Your topic is "The five weeds that make us sneeze." What kinds of visual aids would you use? What materials would you choose for the aids?

2. State four principles for designing visual aids.

3. Describe two advantages visual aids bring to a speech and provide an example of each.

4. Write four guidelines for presenting visual aids.

5. State the advantages and disadvantages of using the chalkboard as a visual aid.

# CHAPTER 9: TRUE-FALSE QUESTIONS

Mark T if the statement is true; F if the statement is false.

_____ 1. Words can shape attitudes.

_____ 2. Language can reflect the speaker's prejudices.

_____ 3. Speakers who use intense language have no need for objective supporting materials.

_____ 4. It is difficult to arouse feelings about events in the remote past.

_____ 5. The audience's apathy is a barrier to the speaker's arousing feelings.

_____ 6. Language can make the future seem real.

_____ 7. Information overload makes it harder for speakers to arouse the feelings of listeners.

_____ 8. Images of heroes are especially important to feelings of group closeness.

_____ 9. A feeling of group closeness automatically makes people want to act.

_____ 10. Whether or not words move listeners to action often depends on the speaker's ethos.

_____ 11. One price of simplification is often distortion.

_____ 12. Hyperbole is a technique that should be used in every speech.

_____ 13. Personification can awaken listeners' feelings.

_____ 14. Speakers should use pronouns like *we* and *our* in speeches to aid identification.

_____ 15. The same tools that can arouse feelings can also incite action.

_____ 16. Rhetorical style is unique to the individual.

_____ 17. One characteristic of good language usage is clarity.

_____ 18. The misuse of a word that sounds like another word is called a malapropism.

# CHAPTER 9: MULTIPLE-CHOICE QUESTIONS

Circle the letter of the *best* answer to each question.

1. Compared to written language, oral language is
   a. more formal
   b. more structured
   c. more colloquial
   d. more deliberated
   e. none of the above

2. Compared to written language, oral language should
   a. use simpler construction
   b. use pauses and vocal emphasis as punctuation
   c. use more repetition
   d. all of the above
   e. none of the above

3. Which of the following is a power of oral language?
   a. to make listeners see
   b. to awaken feelings
   c. to create group identity
   d. to help listeners remember
   e. all of the above

4. The power to make listeners see
   a. affects their awareness of a subject
   b. affects their perception of the world
   c. moves them to action
   d. both a and c
   e. both a and b

5. Which of the following is a barrier that language must overcome to awaken feelings?

    a. time

    b. distance

    c. apathy

    d. all of the above

    e. none of the above

6. Most listeners tend to be

    a. past-oriented

    b. present-oriented

    c. future-oriented

    d. disoriented

    e. easily reoriented

7. A speaker who talks about past heroes to bind a group together is primarily trying to

    a. educate the audience

    b. create a common identity

    c. make listeners see

    d. encourage action

    e. discourage action

8. The power to make us remember refers to

    a. remembering to take action

    b. retention of the message

    c. revival of past memories

    d. rephrasing main points

    e. all of the above

9. Barriers exist between speaker and audience when the subject is

    a. abstract

    b. complex

    c. vast

    d. all of the above

    e. none of the above

10. Which of the following is an abstract word?
    a. pasta
    b. patriotism
    c. rain
    d. brush
    e. football

11. Tools for overcoming abstraction include
    a. culturetypes
    b. stereotypes
    c. similes
    d. all of the above
    e. none of the above

12. Metaphors should be
    a. long
    b. mixed
    c. ostentatious
    d. all of the above
    e. none of the above

13. "Teenage pregnancy is a plague on our nation" is an example of a
    a. simile
    b. metaphor
    c. simplification
    d. hyperbole
    e. metonymy

14. Using part of something to represent the whole is
    a. hyperbole
    b. metaphor
    c. metonymy
    d. synecdoche
    e. onomatopoeia

15. *Buzz* illustrates which linguistic technique?
    a. hyperbole
    b. metaphor
    c. metonymy
    d. synecdoche
    e. onomatopoeia

16. A technique particularly well suited to the arousal of emotion is
    a. hyperbole
    b. synecdoche
    c. onomatopoeia
    d. simplification
    e. simile

17. Giving abstract or inanimate objects human qualities is
    a. onomatopoeia
    b. personification
    c. simile
    d. metonymy
    e. hyperbole

18. Referring to *our* needs involves the use of
    a. an inclusive pronoun
    b. a group narrative
    c. metonymy
    d. a special symbol
    e. personification

19. Imagery based on light and darkness involves
    a. personification
    b. archetypal metaphor
    c. hyperbole
    d. metonymy
    e. special symbols

20. Repetition of the initial sounds in words is
    a. antithesis
    b. archetypes
    c. hyperbole
    d. alliteration
    e. anaphora

21. Using the same initial wording in a sequence of phrases is
    a. alliteration
    b. anaphora
    c. archetypes
    d. onomatopoeia
    e. inversion

22. Strategic repetition is a form of
    a. archetypal metaphor
    b. inversion
    c. amplification
    d. onomatopoeia
    e. personification

## CHAPTER 9: SHORT-ANSWER QUESTIONS

Put the correct answer in each blank.

1. Comparisons using *like* or *as* are called _____.

2. Comparisons using words that normally belong in one arena to designate another are _____.

3. Using part of something to represent the whole is the linguistic device called _____.

4. The use of words that imitate the sounds they represent is _____.

5. Exaggeration to stir emotions is called _____.

6. Attributing human characteristics to inanimate objects is called _____.

7. Images that use universal constants (such as *storm/calm, light/dark*) to anchor a group in its human identity are _____ _____.

NAME _____          SECTION _____

# CHAPTER 9: ESSAY QUESTIONS

Answer each question in detail.

1. Discuss four of the five "C's" of good language use.

2. Write a metaphor that describes how you feel about college.

3. Explain two techniques to make listeners feel.

4. Write a personification about a car or a bicycle.

5. Describe two techniques to create group identity.

# CHAPTER 10: TRUE-FALSE QUESTIONS

Mark T if the statement is true; F if the statement is false.

_____ 1. Effectiveness in public communication is judged by both what you say and how you say it.

_____ 2. A speech is not a speech until it has been presented by the speaker to the audience.

_____ 3. The starting point for effective presentation is the speaker's pitch variety.

_____ 4. An effective presentation calls attention to itself.

_____ 5. A formal, oratorical style characterizes the most effective presentation.

_____ 6. An effective presentation talks *at*, not *with*, people.

_____ 7. You should keep impromptu presentations short.

_____ 8. You should always stand when making impromptu speeches.

_____ 9. Memorized speeches discourage adaptation to an audience.

_____ 10. No part of an extemporaneous speech should ever be memorized.

_____ 11. Manuscript presentation is preferred when split-second timing is necessary.

_____ 12. The exact wording changes each time you give the same extemporaneous speech.

_____ 13. Impromptu presentations are more polished than extemporaneous presentations.

_____ 14. A good speaking voice conveys your meaning fully and clearly in a manner that enhances your ethos.

_____ 15. You should cultivate a good speaking voice for its own sake.

_____ 16. The first step in learning to use your voice more effectively is to evaluate how you usually talk.

_____ 17. When nervous, the average speaker's pitch gets lower.

_____ 18. The slower the rate of speech, the better.

_____ 19. The more volume in your speech, the better.

# CHAPTER 10: MULTIPLE-CHOICE QUESTIONS

Circle the letter of the *best* answer to each question.

1. Public presentation skills are useful in
   a. formal speeches
   b. job interviews
   c. social situations
   d. informal meetings
   e. all of the above

2. The Latin derivative of *communication* means
   a. communist
   b. command
   c. common
   d. consequence
   e. creation

3. An oratorical style
   a. is the best
   b. emphasizes your purpose
   c. detracts from the message
   d. emphasizes the message
   e. none of the above

4. A good speech presentation
   a. is a bit more formal than everyday conversation
   b. sounds spontaneous
   c. is appropriate for the audience
   d. all of the above
   e. none of the above

5. Which of the following is *not* an appropriate method of speech presentation?

   a. impromptu

   b. oratorical

   c. extemporaneous

   d. manuscript

   e. memorized

6. Impromptu speeches involve

   a. rather formal situations

   b. little or no preparation time

   c. an average amount of preparation time

   d. speaking without organization

   e. ghost-written manuscripts

7. For impromptu speeches, you should

   a. never use notes

   b. jot down a few notes in outline form

   c. ignore cues from other speakers

   d. all of the above

   e. none of the above

8. Memorized speeches

   a. are the best type for novices

   b. are good ways to give different audiences the identical message

   c. often sound stilted

   d. all of the above

   e. none of the above

9. Manuscript presentations

   a. require less practice than other forms

   b. should be written in essay style

   c. avoid the main problems of memorized speeches

   d. all of the above

   e. none of the above

10. Reading from a manuscript is preferred when
    a. time is not an important factor
    b. eye contact is not important
    c. accurate wording is imperative
    d. all of the above
    e. none of the above

11. Extemporaneous presentations
    a. are practiced
    b. are prepared in advance
    c. let you adjust to the audience's feedback
    d. all of the above
    e. none of the above

12. Which type of presentation offers the best opportunity to adapt to the audience?
    a. memorized
    b. manuscript
    c. oratorical
    d. extemporaneous
    e. all of the above

13. Pitch refers to the
    a. placement of a voice on the musical scale
    b. speed at which words are uttered
    c. volume of sound
    d. color and variety in articulation
    e. the production of individual sounds and pauses

14. The level at which you usually speak is your
    a. optimum pitch
    b. optimum articulation
    c. habitual rate
    d. habitual pitch
    e. none of the above

15. Serious speech topics call for
    a. a habitual pitch
    b. a more deliberate rate
    c. a greater volume
    d. a higher pitch
    e. a lower pitch

16. Improper breathing can cause
    a. too quiet a voice
    b. too high a pitch
    c. a strident vocal quality
    d. all of the above
    e. none of the above

17. The way you produce individual speech sounds is
    a. pitch
    b. articulation
    c. vocal variety
    d. dialect
    e. pronunciation

18. The correctness with which you say a given word is
    a. pitch
    b. articulation
    c. vocal variety
    d. dialect
    e. pronunciation

19. Where you were raised often is reflected in your
    a. pitch
    b. rate
    c. vocal variety
    d. dialect
    e. articulation

20. In America, trustworthiness is often judged by
    a. articulation standards
    b. eye contact
    c. vocal variety
    d. pitch
    e. both c and d

# CHAPTER 10: SHORT-ANSWER QUESTIONS

Put the correct answer in each blank.

1. Situations where you have little or no preparation time call for _____ speeches.

2. Reading a speech is called _____ presentation.

3. Speeches that are prepared but not written or memorized are called _____.

4. The placement of a voice on the musical scale is called _____.

5. The way you pronounce individual sounds is your _____.

6. The correctness with which you say a given word is its _____.

7. When you reach the podium, you should pause and establish _____ _____ with the audience.

# CHAPTER 10: ESSAY QUESTIONS

Answer each question in detail.

1. Compare and contrast the advantages and disadvantages of memorized and extemporaneous presentations.

2. Describe the preparation and practice procedures for a manuscript presentation.

3. Explain the importance of eye contact and facial expression to overall presentation.

4. Discuss the statement, "Speakers gesture with their whole bodies."

5. Discuss how you should practice presenting a speech.

# CHAPTER 11: TRUE-FALSE QUESTIONS

Mark T if the statement is true; F if the statement is false.

_____ 1. Sharing information was more important to early primates than to us today.

_____ 2. Information is power.

_____ 3. Information is a valuable commodity in our culture.

_____ 4. Informative speeches ask listeners to change beliefs or behaviors.

_____ 5. If you know a subject well enough to satisfy yourself, that will also be enough knowledge to prepare an informative speech.

_____ 6. An informative speech primarily repeats material the audience already knows.

_____ 7. An informative speech shapes listener perceptions.

_____ 8. If listeners don't already have a reason to care about your topic, you should get another topic.

_____ 9. Surprise may be necessary for contrast techniques to be effective.

_____ 10. Gestures and movement comprise the attention-arousing technique of novelty.

_____ 11. When you refer to familiar names and places that have personal meaning for your audience, you are using the attention-arousing device of relevance.

_____ 12. Information is useless unless it is retained.

_____ 13. The more frequently we hear something, the more likely we are to retain it.

_____ 14. If you want your message to be remembered, you must tell listeners how it relates to their lives.

_____ 15. How a message is structured affects how it is retained.

_____ 16. Comparison and contrast designs are particularly good for topics that are new to an audience.

_____ 17. A speech should never mix speech designs.

# CHAPTER 11: MULTIPLE-CHOICE QUESTIONS

Circle the letter of the *best* answer to each question.

1. Information
   a. must be shared across generations for civilization to continue
   b. is important to survival
   c. helps us to live better
   d. all of the above
   e. none of the above

2. "Information is power" means it
   a. helps us control objects
   b. helps us control the environment
   c. helps us control other people
   d. all of the above
   e. none of the above

3. Information is power
   a. always
   b. only when it is shared
   c. over time
   d. all of the above
   e. none of the above

4. Which of the following is a function of informative speech?
   a. recommending options
   b. recommending solutions
   c. shaping perceptions
   d. all of the above
   e. none of the above

5. An informative speech
   a. asks
   b. takes
   c. gives
   d. demands
   e. solicits

6. Which of the following is *not* a main factor in the learning process discussed in the chapter?
   a. perception
   b. motivation
   c. attention
   d. retention
   e. All of the above are basic factors.

7. Which of the following is *not* a factor that sustains attention?
   a. intensity
   b. novelty
   c. activity
   d. relevance
   e. All of the above are factors.

8. Alliteration and anaphora utilize which attention-attracting factor?
   a. novelty
   b. activity
   c. contrast
   d. repetition
   e. intensity

9. Concrete action words and gestures use the attention-arousing device of
   a. novelty
   b. activity
   c. contrast
   d. repetition
   e. intensity

10. Suddenly lowering your volume to make a point uses the attention-getting device of

   a. relevance

   b. activity

   c. contrast

   d. repetition

   e. intensity

11. Referring to familiar places that have personal meaning for the audience utilizes the attention-getting device of

   a. relevance

   b. activity

   c. contrast

   d. repetition

   e. intensity

12. Which of the following is *not* a type of informative speech?

   a. description

   b. demonstration

   c. explanation

   d. examination

   e. All of the above are types of informative speech.

13. A speech that shows the audience how to do something is

   a. descriptive

   b. demonstrative

   c. exclamative

   d. declarative

   e. none of the above

14. Which of the following is *not* a useful design for informative speeches?

   a. spatial

   b. categorical

   c. sequential

   d. comparison and contrast

   e. All of the above are useful designs.

15. Designs arranged by geographic placement are
    a. categorical
    b. comparison and contrast
    c. causation
    d. historical
    e. spatial

16. When you relate something familiar to something unfamiliar, the design is
    a. categorical
    b. comparison and contrast
    c. causation
    d. cause-effect
    e. problem-solution

17. Presenting the chronological steps in a process uses which design?
    a. categorical
    b. causation
    c. historical
    d. sequential
    e. spatial

18. Speeches that try to answer the question *why* use which design?
    a. categorical
    b. causation
    d. historical
    d. sequential
    e. spatial

# CHAPTER 11: SHORT-ANSWER QUESTIONS

Put the correct answer in each blank.

1. A subject having natural divisions may call for a _____ design.

2. Designs based on geographic location are called _____.

3. A comparison of two subjects from the same field is called a _____ analogy.

4. A comparison of subjects from different fields is called a _____ analogy.

5. The organizational design for informative speeches that attempts to answer *why* events occur is called a _____ design.

6. The type of informative speech best suited to present abstract or new ideas is called a speech of _____.

# CHAPTER 11: ESSAY QUESTIONS

Answer each question in detail.

1. Define four organizational designs useful for informative speeches.

2. Discuss the three primary forms of informative speeches.

3. Explain three techniques for arousing and maintaining an audience's attention.

4. Describe how you would make a speech on snake-bite remedies relevant to members of your class.

5. Differentiate between speeches that describe and speeches that explain.

# CHAPTER 12: TRUE-FALSE QUESTIONS

Mark T if the statement is true; F if the statement is false.

_____ 1. Supporting materials are the basic building blocks of speeches.

_____ 2. The burden of support is heavier for informative speeches than for persuasive speeches.

_____ 3. *Information* in speeches only takes the form of facts and testimony.

_____ 4. Interpretation of facts can be a source of distortion.

_____ 5. One source of information is as good as any other as far as audiences are concerned.

_____ 6. It is unwise to combine statistics with other types of proof.

_____ 7. Examples are a means of sustaining audience interest.

_____ 8. Inferential statistics are based on certainty.

_____ 9. It is good to rely solely on one source of information for your facts.

_____ 10. Older statistics are always as good as most recent statistics on the same topics.

_____ 11. Examples enhance the audience's perception of a concept's importance.

_____ 12. A good example reflects the exception to the general trend.

_____ 13. You cannot be an effective speaker without learning to use examples well.

_____ 14. A well-told narrative creates a sense of suspense.

_____ 15. Good use of narration involves dramatic pauses.

_____ 16. Biased sources are best for expert testimony.

_____ 17. Unlike other forms of proof, testimony need not be up to date.

# CHAPTER 12: MULTIPLE-CHOICE QUESTIONS

Circle the letter of the *best* answer to each question.

1. Supporting materials provide
   a. substance
   b. reliability
   c. appeal
   d. all of the above
   e. none of the above

2. Which of the following is *not* a major function of supporting materials?
   a. demonstrate the meaning of subjects
   b. show the relevance of subjects
   c. verify controversial statements
   d. all of the above
   e. none of the above

3. As the speaker interprets facts in a speech, one likely result is
   a. increased speaker credibility
   b. some level of distortion
   c. a lessening of the speech's potential to explain
   d. all of the above
   e. none of the above

4. Data that describe subjects in terms of their magnitude are
   a. facts
   b. inferential statistics
   c. descriptive statistics
   d. expert testimony
   e. expressed statistics

5. When numbers are large or unfamiliar, it is wise to

    a. drop them from your speech

    b. change them so they look more believable

    c. illustrate them with examples the audience can relate to

    d. say them quickly, then move on to something else

    e. all of the above

6. Inferential statistics are based on

    a. probability

    b. certainty

    c. immutable truth

    d. testimony

    e. none of the above

7. When evaluating facts and figures, you should consider all of the following *except*

    a. Are the facts and figures recent?

    b. Are you relying too much on one source?

    c. Are the facts impressive in themselves?

    d. All of the above should be evaluated.

    e. None of the above should be evaluated.

8. Examples may be used to

    a. arouse attention

    b. sustain interest

    c. clarify ideas

    d. personalize the subject

    e. all of the above

9. An example that is fully developed is called a(n)

    a. extended example

    b. brief example

    c. factual example

    d. hypothetical example

    e. hypnotic example

10. Hypothetical examples are
    a. typical of the event being illustrated
    b. composites built from several sources
    c. useful when factual examples are hard to find
    d. all of the above
    e. none of the above

11. Which of the following is *not* a criterion for evaluating an example?
    a. Is it representative?
    b. Is it interesting?
    c. Does it seem plausible?
    d. Is it appropriate?
    e. Is it too short?

12. You should use examples
    a. to clarify abstract concepts
    b. to fill time
    c. to prove a point absolutely
    d. all of the above
    e. none of the above

13. The type of supporting material that tells a *complete* story is a
    a. hypothetical example
    b. factual example
    c. narrative
    d. statistical reference
    e. testimony

14. Which type of supporting material often has its own introduction, body, and conclusion?
    a. hypothetical example
    b. factual example
    c. narrative
    d. statistic
    e. testimony

15. A narrative is effective when
    a. it is not real to the audience
    b. it is representative of the point
    c. it is independent of the speech topic
    d. all of the above
    e. none of the above

16. Narratives should do all of the following *except*
    a. use active verbs
    b. contain dialogue
    c. be economical
    d. have a plot line
    e. rely on abstract language

17. Citing authorities in the area of your subject is using
    a. statistical evidence
    b. lay testimony
    c. prestige testimony
    d. expert testimony
    e. narration

18. Expert testimony is best when
    a. your subject is technical
    b. you identify the expert's credentials
    c. your source is an expert in the field under discussion
    d. all of the above
    e. none of the above

19. When you cite a well-respected person who is not an authority on your subject, you are using
    a. statistics
    b. lay testimony
    c. prestige testimony
    d. expert testimony
    e. narration

20. The purpose of lay testimony is to
    a. fill time
    b. give authenticity to a concept
    c. capitalize on an expert's ethos
    d. all of the above
    e. none of the above

21. All testimony must meet which of the following criteria?
    a. be paraphrased or quoted accurately
    b. come from a published source
    c. come from a well-respected expert
    d. all of the above
    e. none of the above

# CHAPTER 12: SHORT-ANSWER QUESTIONS

Put the correct answer in each blank.

1. _____ statistics talk about subjects in terms of magnitude and distribution.

2. Statistics often demonstrate _____, or relationships between two sets of facts.

3. Statistics can be used to predict changes over time, or _____.

4. When you refer to an event that really happened, you are using a(n) _____ example.

5. Although not real itself, a _____ example is a representation of a real situation.

6. Testimony that uses the exact words of the source is quoting the source _____.

# CHAPTER 12: ESSAY QUESTIONS

Answer each question in detail.

1. List and discuss the strengths and advantages of two types of supporting materials.

2. Discuss three criteria for evaluating examples.

3. Define and differentiate between two kinds of statistics.

4. Discuss three instances where narratives may be particularly useful in a speech.

# CHAPTER 13: TRUE-FALSE QUESTIONS

Mark T if the statement is true; F if the statement is false.

_____ 1. The right to persuade is the cornerstone of our social and political system.

_____ 2. The right to persuade is guaranteed by the First Amendment to the Constitution.

_____ 3. The ethical obligation is larger for persuasive speeches than for informative speeches.

_____ 4. Informative speaking calls for more audience commitment than persuasive speaking.

_____ 5. Persuasion often requires group action for its success.

_____ 6. Every member of your audience is automatically exposed to your message.

_____ 7. Persuasion is effective only if there is total audience commitment.

_____ 8. Demonstrating the new behavior is an important element in McGuire's integration step.

_____ 9. Enticing a hostile audience to listen does not involve persuasion.

_____ 10. Analysis of the audience is vital to persuasion.

_____ 11. Attitudes and beliefs are relatively easy to change.

_____ 12. The more important a belief is to the receiver, the less likely it is that he or she will change it.

_____ 13. If opposition to your position seems insurmountable, you should always state your proposal, even though you're sure it will be rejected.

_____ 14. Using humor is often an effective way to disarm hostile audiences.

_____ 15. Sometimes recognizing and stating the differences between the speaker's and audience's viewpoints can establish trust.

_____ 16. You should try to move the audience toward your position in a series of small steps, rather than in one grand leap.

_____ 17. Listeners' reluctance to commit themselves often comes from a lack of information.

_____ 18. Speeches addressing attitudes can aim for a total change of conviction.

_____ 19. Speeches of contention should never confront the opposition's views directly.

_____ 20. You should use only positive analogies, according to the analogy design.

# CHAPTER 13: MULTIPLE-CHOICE QUESTIONS

Circle the letter of the *best* answer to each question.

1. Deliberation occurs when
   a. all sides of an issue are examined in free and open debate
   b. decisions are imposed on us
   c. persuaders present one side of an issue
   d. all of the above
   e. none of the above

2. Exposure to different viewpoints is
   a. abominable
   b. bad because individuals are easily persuaded
   c. good because better decisions are produced
   d. irrelevant to the persuasion process
   e. irrelevant because the outcome is usually the same

3. In contrast to informative speaking, persuasive speaking
   a. reveals and clarifies options
   b. asks the speaker to act as a teacher
   c. stresses understanding
   d. all of the above
   e. none of the above

4. McGuire's steps in the persuasion process include
   a. orientation
   b. acceptance
   c. integration
   d. all of the above
   e. none of the above

5. Which of the following is an element in McGuire's category of reception?

    a. orientation

    b. acceptance

    c. integration

    d. involvement

    e. comprehension

6. Which of the following is a factor in McGuire's orientation step?

    a. exposure

    b. involvement

    c. comprehension

    d. reception

    e. integration

7. Which of the following is an element in McGuire's acceptance step?

    a. agreement

    b. retention

    c. remembering agreement

    d. all of the above

    e. none of the above

8. Attitudes and beliefs are

    a. never changed

    b. hard to change

    c. easy to change

    d. not relevant to persuasion

    e. surface values

9. When confronting a hostile audience, the first thing to do is

    a. make them defensive

    b. establish good will

    c. use emotional appeals

    d. criticize their position

    e. confront their values

10. Which of the following is *not* one of the steps in Simons's co-active approach?
    a. Start with areas of agreement.
    b. Establish mutually acceptable values or principles.
    c. Use unrecognizable sources.
    d. Use humor.
    e. Use multisided presentations.

11. Which of the following is most effective for persuading a hostile audience?
    a. hard-hitting advocacy of your position
    b. a singlesided presentation
    c. a multisided presentation
    d. inflammatory language to polarize listeners
    e. none of the above

12. When your speech results in increased opposition to your position, which phenomenon has occurred.
    a. reverse polarity
    b. great expectation fallacy
    c. sleeper effect
    d. boomerang effect
    e. consciousness-raising function

13. Hoping for too much change from a one-shot message is called
    a. reverse polarity
    b. great expectation fallacy
    c. sleeper effect
    d. boomerang effect
    e. consciousness-raising function

14. A delayed reaction that occurs only after the audience has integrated your message is called
    a. reverse polarity
    b. great expectation fallacy
    c. sleeper effect
    d. boomerang effect
    e. consciousness-raising function

15. A speech that attempts to persuade students to picket the administration building is a

   a. speech of explanation

   b. speech urging action

   c. speech of contention

   d. speech addressing attitudes

   e. none of the above

16. The motivated sequence design was introduced by

   a. Simons

   b. McGuire

   c. Monroe

   d. Osborn

   e. McCorkle

17. Which of the following is *not* a step in the motivated sequence design?

   a. arouse attention

   b. diffuse hostility

   c. demonstrate need

   d. satisfy the need

   e. visualize the result

18. The design that points out inconsistencies in the position of the opposition is

   a. problem-solution

   b. analogy

   c. motivated sequence

   d. hostile audience

   e. refutative

# CHAPTER 13: SHORT-ANSWER QUESTIONS

Put the correct answer in each blank.

1. When listeners end up with the opposite opinion of what you intended, a _____ effect has occurred.

2. When listeners move closer to your viewpoint after a time delay, a _____ effect has occurred.

3. Wanting too much change from a single persuasive message commits the _____ _____ fallacy.

4. The organizational pattern that tells listeners both what is wrong and how to fix it is the _____-_____ design.

5. A negative _____ design might compare an event the speaker wishes discontinued with something disliked by the audience.

6. Monroe's organizational design is called the _____ _____.

7. When the speaker tries to counteract or even destroy the claims of the opposition, the _____ design is being used.

# CHAPTER 13: ESSAY QUESTIONS

Answer each question in detail.

1. Define two speech designs particularly useful in persuasive speaking.

2. Explain Monroe's motivated sequence.

3. Describe what happens when the boomerang effect occurs.

4. State which organizational pattern you would use to convince listeners that horse racing is or is not desirable. Also state why this design best suits your purpose.

5. Differentiate between speeches addressing attitudes and speeches of contention.

# CHAPTER 14: TRUE-FALSE QUESTIONS

Mark T if the statement is true; F if the statement is false.

_____ 1. Supporting materials can be used as evidence.

_____ 2. Persuasion asks the audience to take a risk.

_____ 3. Testimony is even more critical as proof in persuasive speeches than in informative speeches.

_____ 4. The more you ask of listeners, the more proof you must provide.

_____ 5. Currency of information is not as important in persuasive speeches as in informative speeches.

_____ 6. It is best to rely on one primary source during persuasive speeches.

_____ 7. Good reasons are based on generally accepted values and practices.

_____ 8. The study of proofs is a relatively new part of communication studies.

_____ 9. Persuasive speeches usually rely solely on one type of proof.

_____ 10. Proof by logos assumes people act rationally most of the time.

_____ 11. Charitable organizations often use ethos as their primary persuasive appeal.

_____ 12. Proof by pathos assumes people are moved by emotion.

_____ 13. In attempting to persuade Congress to provide aid to the Contras in Nicaragua, Reagan found pathos more effective in the long run than logos.

_____ 14. People can be authoritative sources, but books cannot.

_____ 15. You should use only one form of proof during a speech.

_____ 16. Audiences always accept a syllogism's major premise without question.

_____ 17. Definition of terms is an important starting point for some arguments.

_____ 18. Argument by perspective sometimes uses metaphors.

_____ 19. "The sky is blue, so we should go to a movie" is a *non sequitur*.

# CHAPTER 14: MULTIPLE-CHOICE QUESTIONS

Circle the letter of the *best* answer to each question.

1. In persuasive speeches, the primary function of evidence is to
    a. illustrate and clarify points
    b. add interest to otherwise dry facts
    c. justify what the listener is asked to accept
    d. all of the above
    e. none of the above

2. Which type of example is most powerful in persuasion?
    a. hypothetical
    b. factual
    c. narrative
    d. representative
    e. all of the above

3. Lay testimony in persuasive speeches functions best
    a. as a primary support
    b. to emphasize values
    c. to relate your subject to your listeners' lives and experiences
    d. all of the above
    e. none of the above

4. Admirable good reasons
    a. represent values like honesty and courage
    b. suggest we should do something because it will help us
    c. suggest we should do something because it is our duty
    d. all of the above
    e. none of the above

5. We should evaluate evidence based on its
   a. relevance
   b. consequences
   c. consistency
   d. all of the above
   e. none of the above

6. Proof based on emotion is called
   a. ethos
   b. pathos
   c. logos
   d. ethics
   e. mythos

7. Appeals to mythos are based on
   a. rational evidence
   b. motives or emotions
   c. personal character
   d. traditions and identities of a group
   e. all of the above

8. Which of the following is part of a proof by logos?
   a. statement
   b. evidence
   c. claim
   d. qualifier
   e. all of the above

9. Proof by pathos assumes that people
   a. make rational decisions
   b. make decisions based on their cultural heritage
   c. make decisions emotionally
   d. all of the above
   e. none of the above

10. Heavy use of pathos can
    a. make the message more credible
    b. make the audience suspicious
    c. reduce the need for logos
    d. reduce the need for ethics
    e. reduce the need for mythos

11. Proof by ethos assumes that people
    a. make rational decisions
    b. make decisions based on their cultural heritage
    c. make decisions emotionally
    d. all of the above
    e. none of the above

12. In proof by ethos, you must be concerned about
    a. your personal credibility
    b. the credibility of the audience
    c. the credibility of your sources
    d. all of the above
    e. a and c only

13. Listeners evaluate your sources in terms of their
    a. competence
    b. attractiveness
    c. power
    d. integrity
    e. all of the above

14. Proof by mythos assumes people make decisions
    a. rationally
    b. based on their cultural heritage
    c. emotionally
    d. based on authoritative testimony
    e. none of the above

15. Proof by mythos helps the audience see
    a. who else supports the speaker's position
    b. the logic of the speaker's position
    c. how the speaker's position fits the group's tradition
    d. if the proposal feels like a good idea
    e. all of the above

16. Quoting a respected authority in the field provides proof by
    a. logos
    b. ethos
    c. pathos
    d. mythos
    e. all of the above

17. Suggesting that battered women will have nowhere to go if the shelter program doesn't get enough donations is proof by
    a. logos
    b. ethos
    c. pathos
    d. mythos
    e. all of the above

18. Referring to the "Spirit of '76" provides proof by
    a. logos
    b. ethos
    c. pathos
    d. mythos
    e. all of the above

19. Reasoning that moves from an accepted truth to specific conclusions is
    a. major premise
    b. minor premise
    c. conclusive
    d. deductive
    e. inductive

20. Arguments that begin with specific facts and proceed to more general conclusions are
    a. major premise
    b. minor premise
    c. conclusive
    d. deductive
    e. inductive

21. Arguments focusing on whether the unborn fetus is organic matter or a human being use which of the following?
    a. deductive reasoning
    b. inductive reasoning
    c. argument by definition
    d. argument by perspective
    e. argument by metaphor

22. Assuming that marijuana smoking will lead to cocaine use and eventual addiction commits a(n)
    a. red herring fallacy
    b. misuse of fact
    c. *post hoc ergo propter hoc* fallacy
    d. *ad hominem* fallacy
    e. slippery slope fallacy

23. Calling the opponents of plastic handgun regulations "gun nuts" is a(n)
    a. red herring argument
    b. misuse of fact
    c. *post hoc ergo propter hoc* fallacy
    d. *ad hominem* argument
    e. slippery slope fallacy

24. Assuming Reagan was the one who freed the U.S. hostages in Iran because the release took place after he was inaugurated commits a(n)
    a. red herring fallacy
    b. misuse of fact
    c. *post hoc ergo propter hoc* fallacy
    d. *ad hominem* fallacy
    e. slippery slope fallacy

# CHAPTER 14: SHORT-ANSWER QUESTIONS

Put the correct answer in each blank.

1. Aristotle called proofs based on rational evidence _____.

2. Aristotle called proofs based on motives or emotion _____.

3. Aristotle called proofs based on the personal character of the source _____.

4. The authors call proofs based on cultural heritage _____.

5. The basic three-part pattern of deductive reasoning is called a _____.

6. Reasoning based on analogies is called argument by _____.

7. Using averages to represent total reality commits the illusion of the average, or myth of the _____.

# CHAPTER 14: ESSAY QUESTIONS

Answer each question in detail.

1. Write a syllogism about trees; label its parts.

2. Differentiate between inductive and deductive reasoning.

3. Name and define any two fallacies.

4. Identify and define Aristotle's three types of proof.

5. Explain the concept of mythos and how it functions as proof.

# CHAPTER 15: TRUE-FALSE QUESTIONS

Mark T if the statement is true; F if the statement is false.

_____ 1. Ceremonial speaking helps people sustain a sense of purpose and continuity.

_____ 2. Most techniques for ceremonial speeches are quite different from the techniques discussed in previous chapters.

_____ 3. Identification is one of the major techniques for ceremonial speeches.

_____ 4. Many ceremonies are times for renewal of commitment to a group.

_____ 5. Anaphora can help magnify ideas.

_____ 6. Metaphor can help magnify ideas.

_____ 7. It is appropriate to list all your accomplishments in a speech of introduction.

_____ 8. A speech of introduction should be quite lengthy.

_____ 9. Accomplishments of others serve as important social symbols.

_____ 10. A speech of tribute should mention some of your own accomplishments, as well as those of the person being honored.

_____ 11. The average person is not likely to be called on to make a toast.

_____ 12. "Here's to Joe—a great guy" is an adequate toast for most occasions.

_____ 13. Toasting is an important social ritual that often signals an important change or accomplishment.

_____ 14. Toasts should be spontaneous rather than preplanned.

_____ 15. A short toast is one of the few public presentations you should memorize.

_____ 16. When receiving an award, you should make a speech of acceptance that recaps your accomplishments.

_____ 17. Jokes are usually appropriate for acceptance speeches.

_____ 18. An inspirational speech may be commercial or political.

_____ 19. The after-dinner speech is one of the great traditions of American public speaking.

_____ 20. Humor is an integral part of most after-dinner speeches.

# CHAPTER 15: MULTIPLE-CHOICE QUESTIONS

Circle the letter of the *best* answer to each question.

1. The type of speaking that helps people gain appreciation of themselves through an awareness of their common heritage is

   a. informative

   b. persuasive

   c. motivational

   d. ceremonial

   e. all of the above

2. Ceremonial speaking may

   a. establish ethical standards

   b. establish a moral basis for action

   c. contribute to the integration phase of persuasion

   d. all of the above

   e. none of the above

3. Which of the following is a technique basic to ceremonial speaking?

   a. categorical imprecision

   b. causal fallacy

   c. parallelism

   d. magnification

   e. subordination

4. Which of the following is *not* an identification technique?

   a. narration

   b. metaphor and simile

   c. hero/heroine recognition

   d. renewal of group commitment

   e. All are identification techniques.

5. When you refer to individuals who have succeeded beyond expectation, you are using the identification appeal of
   a. revitalization
   b. renewal of group commitment
   c. hero/heroine recognition
   d. simile
   e. magnification

6. Selecting a feature to emphasize as representation of the values you are discussing is
   a. identification
   b. magnification
   c. hero/heroine recognition
   d. metaphor
   e. narration

7. Which of the following is *not* a theme to use when magnifying the positive actions of a person?
   a. ease of accomplishment
   b. overcoming great obstacles
   c. unusual accomplishment
   d. pure motives
   e. all of the above

8. Which of the following is *not* a speech of celebration?
   a. speech of introduction
   b. toast
   c. after-dinner
   d. speech of tribute
   e. All of the above are speeches of celebration.

9. Which of the following is *not* a purpose of the speech of introduction?
   a. strengthening the ethos of the person you are introducing
   b. strengthening your own ethos
   c. tuning the audience to the message that is to follow
   d. laying the groundwork for speaker-audience identification
   e. All of the above are purposes.

10. Tuning the audience in a speech of introduction means you should
    a. preview the speaker's main points
    b. use the speaker's opening lines
    c. use humor very similar to that of the speaker
    d. all of the above
    e. none of the above

11. Celebrating the accomplishments of a person takes which speech form?
    a. introduction
    b. toast
    c. tribute
    d. roast
    e. acceptance

12. Which of the following is *not* a guideline for speeches of tribute?
    a. exaggerate the person's accomplishments
    b. don't focus on yourself
    c. create graphic images of the accomplishment
    d. be sincere
    e. illustrate the values underlying the accomplishment

13. Toasts should
    a. be spontaneous
    b. be long
    c. mention both positive and negative traits
    d. all of the above
    e. none of the above

14. Acceptance speeches should
    a. express gratitude
    b. acknowledge those who made the accomplishment possible
    c. focus on the values of the award
    d. all of the above
    e. none of the above

15. To awaken or reawaken the audience to an important goal, you would use a
    a. speech of introduction
    b. speech of inspiration
    c. speech of tribute
    d. toast
    e. speech of acceptance

16. Inspirational speeches should be
    a. enthusiastic
    b. abstract
    c. self-promoting
    d. funny
    e. all of the above

17. An after-dinner speech is a type of speech to
    a. introduce
    b. inspire
    c. inform
    d. celebrate
    e. accept

18. After-dinner speeches should be
    a. serious
    b. complex
    c. abstract
    d. all of the above
    e. none of the above

19. Humor requires
    a. planning
    b. caution
    c. a purpose
    d. all of the above
    e. none of the above

20. Racist humor is

    a.  acceptable if you are careful that no reporters are present

    b.  acceptable when the audience is racist

    c.  acceptable if most of the audience is racist

    d.  acceptable as long as you don't really mean it

    e.  never acceptable

21. The best kind of humor is often

    a.  an old familiar joke

    b.  your favorite joke

    c.  poking fun at yourself

    d.  poking fun at the audience

    e.  sexist

# CHAPTER 15: SHORT-ANSWER QUESTIONS

Put the correct answer in each blank.

1. Creating ties between the speaker and audience, or _____, is one of two important techniques for ceremonial speaking.

2. Enlarging concepts, or _____, is an important technique of ceremonial speaking.

3. Praising someone else may be part of a speech of _____, a speech of _____, or a _____.

4. Upon receiving an award, you may be called upon to give a speech of _____.

5. The ceremonial speech most tied to banquets and American tradition is the _____ speech.

6. Veterans Day would call for a speech of _____.

# CHAPTER 15: ESSAY QUESTIONS

Answer each question in detail.

1. Explain the two main techniques used in ceremonial speaking.

2. Describe a function that the speech of introduction *should* serve and one it *should not* serve.

3. Describe what should be in an acceptance speech.

4. Identify two occasions well suited for a speech of inspiration.

5. Name two occasions appropriate for a speech of celebration.

NAME _____          SECTION _____

# APPENDIX A: TRUE-FALSE QUESTIONS

Mark T if the statement is true; F if the statement is false.

_____ 1. The authors feel that two-person problem-solving groups can minimize the risk of listening to just one person.

_____ 2. A group approach encourages more open examination of issues than does public confrontation.

_____ 3. Groupthink is a positive characteristic of group activities.

_____ 4. The first step in the problem-solving process is generating solutions.

_____ 5. It is acceptable to proceed with solution brainstorming even if the problem's causes are not fully understood.

_____ 6. Brainstorming sessions involve intense evaluation of each suggestion as it is given.

_____ 7. You should never consider cost when evaluating options.

_____ 8. Once a group has decided on a solution, the next step is to work out the sequence of steps needed to implement the solution.

_____ 9. A group's problem-solving responsibilities stop once the solution is implemented.

_____ 10. An agenda is a meeting plan.

# APPENDIX A: MULTIPLE-CHOICE QUESTIONS

Circle the letter of the *best* answer to each question.

1. Executives spend how many hours per year in group activities?

   a. 50 to 70

   b. 100 to 125

   c. 200 to 300

   d. 500 to 700

   e. over 1000

2. Domination by one group member can result in the development of a single, un-critical frame of mind, known as

   a. parliamentary procedure

   b. parliamentary think

   c. problem-solving process

   d. brainstorming

   e. groupthink

3. Groups can be made more efficient by using which of the following?

   a. parliamentary thinking

   b. risky-shift thinking

   c. problem-solving processes

   d. groupthink

   e. any of the above

4. Which of the following is not a question relevant to the first step of the problem-solving process?

   a. What solutions could solve this issue?

   b. What is the nature of the problem?

   c. Why has the problem occurred?

   d. Who is affected by the problem?

   e. Would things really be better if the problem were solved?

5. A good meeting leader
   a. asks each member to contribute information and opinions
   b. helps get conflict out in the open
   c. keeps the discussion focused on the subject
   d. encourages objective criticism
   e. all of the above

6. Which of the following is *not* a rule for brainstorming sessions?
   a. a recorder should write down each idea
   b. members may pass rather than offer ideas
   c. no idea criticized, no matter how far-fetched
   d. All of the above are rules.
   e. None of the above are rules.

7. Which of the following is *not* a criterion for evaluating possible solutions?
   a. cost
   b. difficulty
   c. additional benefits
   d. additional problems
   e. All of the above are criteria.

8. During the evaluation phase, discussion should focus on
   a. personal profits
   b. ideas
   c. personalities
   d. groupthink
   e. none of the above

9. If the selected solution falls prey to insurmountable obstacles, the group should
   a. give up
   b. redefine the problem so the solution fits
   c. try another solution
   d. go ahead anyway
   e. get a new group leader

10. Group members should be
    a. effective listeners
    b. effective speakers
    c. effective researchers
    d. all of the above
    e. none of the above

11. Behavior that moves a group toward its stated goal is called _____ leadership.
    a. team
    b. task
    c. social
    d. special
    e. parliamentary

12. Behavior that helps the group maintain a good working relationship among members is called _____ leadership.
    a. team
    b. task
    c. social
    d. special
    e. parliamentary

13. If you wish to vote on an issue in formal meetings you must
    a. make a motion
    b. amend a motion
    c. table a motion
    d. call the previous question
    e. move to adjourn

14. One way to stop consideration of an issue before a vote is taken in a formal meeting is to
    a. make a motion
    b. amend a motion
    c. table a motion
    d. call the previous question
    e. move to adjourn

# APPENDIX A: SHORT-ANSWER QUESTIONS

Put the correct answer in each blank.

1. The development of a single, uncritical frame of mind in a group is called _____.

2. _____ is a technique to produce multiple ideas while deferring evaluation of their quality.

3. _____ leadership skills help the group move toward its stated goals.

4. _____ leadership skills help build positive relationships among group members.

5. Formal meetings are conducted under the rules of _____ procedure.

# APPENDIX A: ESSAY QUESTIONS

Answer each question in detail.

    1. Describe the communication skills of an effective group member.

    2. Describe the communication skills of an effective group leader.

    3. Discuss the steps in the group problem-solving process.

*Part V*

# ANSWER KEYS FOR TEST QUESTIONS

# Chapter 1

## Public Speaking As Communication

### True or False

| | | | | |
|---|---|---|---|---|
| 1. T | 2. T | 3. T | 4. T | 5. T |
| 6. F | 7. F | 8. T | 9. F | 10. T |
| 11. F | 12. F | 13. F | 14. T | 15. T |
| 16. F | 17. F | 18. F | | |

### Multiple Choice

| | | | | |
|---|---|---|---|---|
| 1. b | 2. a | 3. c | 4. e | 5. d |
| 6. b | 7. d | 8. a | 9. e | 10. e |
| 11. d | 12. a | 13. c | 14. d | 15. d |
| 16. e | 17. d | 18. b | 19. d | 20. d |
| 21. d | 22. c | 23. d | 24. b | |

### Short Answer

| | | |
|---|---|---|
| 1. first amendment | 2. dynamic circle | 3. source |
| 4. medium | 5. receivers | 6. environment |
| 7. Aristotle | | |

# Chapter 2

## Your First Speech

### True or False

| | | | | |
|---|---|---|---|---|
| 1. T | 2. F | 3. T | 4. T | 5. F |
| 6. F | 7. T | 8. F | 9. T | 10. F |
| 11. T | 12. F | 13. F | 14. F | 15. F |
| 16. F | 17. F | | | |

### Multiple Choice

| | | | | |
|---|---|---|---|---|
| 1. e | 2. b | 3. e | 4. e | 5. c |
| 6. b | 7. d | 8. c | 9. c | 10. c |
| 11. a | 12. c | 13. d | 14. e | 15. e |
| 16. e | 17. a | 18. c | | |

## Short Answer
1. integrity            2. conferred              3. thematic
4. key word             5. cognitive restructuring  6. identification
7. extemporaneous

# Chapter 3

**Critical Listening and Speech Evaluation**

## True or False
1. T          2. T          3. F          4. F          5. F
6. T          7. F          8. T          9. T          10. T
11. T         12. T         13. T         14. F         15. T
16. T         17. F         18. F

## Multiple Choice
1. d          2. a          3. c          4. e          5. d
6. d          7. d          8. e          9. e          10. a
11. b         12. e         13. a         14. d         15. d
16. e         17. a         18. e         19. c         20. d
21. c         22. c         23. a

## Short Answer
1. critical             2. denotative             3. connotative
4. trigger              5. critique, evaluate

# Chapter 4

**Selecting and Researching Your Topic**

## True or False
1. F          2. T          3. F          4. T          5. T
6. F          7. F          8. T          9. F          10. F
11. F         12. F         13. F         14. F         15. F
16. T         17. F         18. T

## Multiple Choice

| | | | | |
|---|---|---|---|---|
| 1. b | 2. e | 3. c | 4. c | 5. d |
| 6. e | 7. d | 8. b | 9. d | 10. c |
| 11. d | 12. d | 13. d | 14. b | 15. e |
| 16. a | 17. d | 18. c | 19. d | 20. e |

## Short Answer

1. specific purpose    2. general    3. specific
4. thematic statement    5. mirror questions

# Chapter 5

## Audience Analysis and Adaptation

## True or False

| | | | | |
|---|---|---|---|---|
| 1. T | 2. T | 3. F | 4. F | 5. T |
| 6. F | 7. T | 8. F | 9. F | 10. T |
| 11. F | 12. F | 13. T | 14. F | 15. T |
| 16. F | 17. F | 18. T | 19. F | |

## Multiple Choice

| | | | | |
|---|---|---|---|---|
| 1. a | 2. d | 3. b | 4. d | 5. c |
| 6. a | 7. d | 8. e | 9. a | 10. e |
| 11. b | 12. d | 13. c | 14. d | 15. b |
| 16. d | 17. c | 18. b | 19. c | 20. d |

## Short Answer

1. context    2. preliminary tuning    3. demographic
4. stereotyping    5. sexist    6. archetypal images

# Chapter 6

## Structuring Your Speech

## True or False

| | | | | |
|---|---|---|---|---|
| 1. T | 2. T | 3. T | 4. T | 5. F |
| 6. F | 7. T | 8. F | 9. T | 10. T |

11. F        12. T        13. T        14. F        15. F
16. T        17. T        18. F

## Multiple Choice
1. d         2. a         3. d         4. c         5. c
6. b         7. b         8. c         9. c         10. a
11. b        12. c        13. d        14. d        15. b
16. d        17. c        18. b        19. e

## Short Answer
1. symmetry          2. internal summary          3. preview
4. historical        5. rhetorical                6. closure
7. spatial

# Chapter 7
## Outlining Your Speech

## True or False
1. T         2. T         3. T         4. T         5. T
6. T         7. T         8. F         9. T         10. F
11. T        12. F        13. T        14. F        15. F
16. F

## Multiple Choice
1. c         2. c         3. d         4. a         5. d
6. d         7. c         8. d         9. c         10. d
11. b        12. d        13. c        14. c        15. b
16. d        17. c        18. c        19. b

## Short Answer
1. subpoints         2. coordination          3. subordination
4. parallel          5. key word              6. preparation

## Chapter 8

**Visual Aids**

**True or False**

| | | | | |
|---|---|---|---|---|
| 1. T | 2. F | 3. F | 4. T | 5. F |
| 6. T | 7. F | 8. F | 9. T | 10. F |
| 11. T | 12. F | 13. T | 14. T | 15. T |
| 16. T | | | | |

**Multiple Choice**

| | | | | |
|---|---|---|---|---|
| 1. d | 2. a | 3. a | 4. d | 5. c |
| 6. d | 7. a | 8. d | 9. d | 10. d |
| 11. d | 12. d | 13. d | 14. a | 15. d |

**Short Answer**

1. monochromatic    2. analogous    3. complementary
4. pie    5. line

## Chapter 9

**The Speaker's Language**

**True or False**

| | | | | |
|---|---|---|---|---|
| 1. T | 2. T | 3. F | 4. T | 5. T |
| 6. T | 7. T | 8. T | 9. F | 10. T |
| 11. T | 12. F | 13. T | 14. T | 15. T |
| 16. T | 17. T | 18. T | | |

**Multiple Choice**

| | | | | |
|---|---|---|---|---|
| 1. c | 2. d | 3. e | 4. e | 5. d |
| 6. b | 7. b | 8. c | 9. d | 10. b |
| 11. c | 12. e | 13. b | 14. d | 15. e |
| 16. a | 17. b | 18. a | 19. b | 20. d |
| 21. b | 22. c | | | |

**Short Answer**

1. similes    2. metaphors    3. synecdoche
4. onomatopoeia    5. hyperbole    6. personification
7. archetypypal metaphors

# Chapter 10

## Presenting Your Speech

### True or False

| | | | | |
|---|---|---|---|---|
| 1. T | 2. T | 3. F | 4. F | 5. F |
| 6. F | 7. T | 8. F | 9. T | 10. F |
| 11. T | 12. T | 13. F | 14. T | 15. F |
| 16. T | 17. F | 18. F | 19. F | |

### Multiple Choice

| | | | | |
|---|---|---|---|---|
| 1. e | 2. c | 3. c | 4. d | 5. b |
| 6. b | 7. b | 8. c | 9. e | 10. c |
| 11. d | 12. d | 13. a | 14. d | 15. b |
| 16. d | 17. b | 18. e | 19. d | 20. b |

### Short Answer

1. impromptu
2. manuscript
3. extemporaneous
4. pitch
5. articulation
6. pronounciation
7. eye contact

# Chapter 11

## The Nature and Kinds of Informative Speaking

### True or False

| | | | | |
|---|---|---|---|---|
| 1. F | 2. T | 3. T | 4. F | 5. F |
| 6. F | 7. T | 8. F | 9. T | 10. F |
| 11. T | 12. T | 13. T | 14. T | 15. T |
| 16. T | 17. F | | | |

### Multiple Choice

| | | | | |
|---|---|---|---|---|
| 1. d | 2. d | 3. b | 4. c | 5. c |
| 6. a | 7. e | 8. d | 9. b | 10. c |
| 11. a | 12. d | 13. b | 14. e | 15. e |
| 16. b | 17. d | 18. b | | |

### Short Answer

1. categorical
2. spatial
3. literal
4. figurative
5. causation
6. explanation

# Chapter 12

## The Use of Supporting Materials

### True or False
| | | | | |
|---|---|---|---|---|
| 1. T | 2. F | 3. F | 4. T | 5. F |
| 6. F | 7. T | 8. F | 9. F | 10. F |
| 11. T | 12. F | 13. T | 14. T | 15. T |
| 16. F | 17. F | | | |

### Multiple Choice
| | | | | |
|---|---|---|---|---|
| 1. d | 2. d | 3. b | 4. c | 5. c |
| 6. a | 7. d | 8. e | 9. a | 10. a |
| 11. e | 12. a | 13. c | 14. c | 15. b |
| 16. e | 17. d | 18. d | 19. c | 20. b |
| 21. a | | | | |

### Short Answer
1. inferential
2. correlations
3. trend
4. factual
5. hypothetical
6. verbatim

# Chapter 13

## The Nature and Kinds of Persuasive Speaking

### True or False
| | | | | |
|---|---|---|---|---|
| 1. T | 2. T | 3. T | 4. F | 5. T |
| 6. F | 7. F | 8. T | 9. F | 10. T |
| 11. F | 12. T | 13. F | 14. T | 15. T |
| 16. T | 17. T | 18. T | 19. F | 20. F |

### Multiple Choice
| | | | | |
|---|---|---|---|---|
| 1. a | 2. c | 3. e | 4. d | 5. d |
| 6. c | 7. d | 8. b | 9. b | 10. c |
| 11. c | 12. d | 13. b | 14. c | 15. b |
| 16. c | 17. b | 18. e | | |

### Short Answer
1. boomerang
2. sleeper
3. great expectation
4. problem solution
5. analogy
6. motivated sequence
7. refutative

# Chapter 14

**Evidence, Proof, and Argument**

## True or False

| | | | | |
|---|---|---|---|---|
| 1. T | 2. T | 3. T | 4. T | 5. F |
| 6. F | 7. T | 8. F | 9. F | 10. T |
| 11. F | 12. T | 13. F | 14. F | 15. F |
| 16. F | 17. T | 18. T | 19. T | |

## Multiple Choice

| | | | | |
|---|---|---|---|---|
| 1. c | 2. b | 3. c | 4. a | 5. d |
| 6. b | 7. d | 8. e | 9. c | 10. b |
| 11. e | 12. e | 13. e | 14. b | 15. c |
| 16. b | 17. c | 18. d | 19. d | 20. e |
| 21. c | 22. e | 23. d | 24. c | |

## Short Answer

| | | |
|---|---|---|
| 1. logos | 2. pathos | 3. ethos |
| 4. mythos | 5. syllogism | 6. perspective |
| 7. mean | | |

# Chapter 15

**Ceremonial Speaking**

## True or False

| | | | | |
|---|---|---|---|---|
| 1. T | 2. F | 3. T | 4. T | 5. T |
| 6. T | 7. F | 8. F | 9. T | 10. F |
| 11. F | 12. F | 13. T | 14. F | 15. T |
| 16. F | 17. F | 18. T | 19. T | 20. T |

## Multiple Choice

| | | | | |
|---|---|---|---|---|
| 1. d | 2. d | 3. d | 4. b | 5. c |
| 6. b | 7. a | 8. e | 9. b | 10. e |
| 11. c | 12. a | 13. e | 14. d | 15. b |
| 16. a | 17. d | 18. e | 19. d | 20. e |
| 21. c | | | | |

## Short Answer

1. identification     2. magnification     3. introduction, tribute, toast
4. acceptance     5. after-dinner     6. tribute

# Appendix A

## Group Communication

### True or False

| 1. F | 2. T | 3. F | 4. F | 5. F |
|------|------|------|------|------|
| 6. F | 7. F | 8. T | 9. F | 10. T |

### Multiple Choice

| 1. d | 2. e | 3. c | 4. a | 5. e |
|------|------|------|------|------|
| 6. d | 7. e | 8. b | 9. c | 10. d |
| 11. b | 12. c | 13. d | 14. c | |

### Short Answer

1. groupthink     2. brainstorming     3. task
4. social     5. parliamentary

*Part VI*

# TRANSPARENCY PACKAGE

Available at no charge to adopters of PUBLIC SPEAKING is a package of 19 acetate transparencies for use with an overhead projector. To order a set, please contact your local Houghton Mifflin representative or regional office.

## LIST OF TRANSPARENCIES

### Speaker's Notes

1. How to Create a Good Public Speech (Chapter 1)

2. Questions to Ask Yourself for an Introductory Speech (Chapter 2)

3. Questions for Finding a Specific Purpose (Chapter 4)

4. Questions to Ask About the Occasion and Audience (Chapter 5)

5. Capturing the Attention of Your Audience (Chapter 6)

6. The Five C's of Effective Language Use (Chapter 9)

7. Practicing with an Outline (Chapter 10)

8. Using Facts and Statistics (Chapter 12)

9. Using Examples (Chapter 12)

10. Using Narratives (Chapter 12)

11. Using Testimony (Chapter 12)

12. Using Evidence (Chapter 14)

13. Developing Speeches of Tribute (Chapter 15)

14. Making a Toast (Chapter 15)

### Text Figures

15. Figure 1.1 Communication as a Dynamic Circle

16. Figure 14.2 Examples of Defective Evidence

### Model Visual Aids

17. Figure 8.1 A Map of Yellowstone Park

18. Figure 8.2 College Degrees Conferred by Gender, 1950 and 1983

19. Figure 8.6 Flip Chart Explanation of an Acronym

# APPENDIXES

**Appendix A:** Sample Introductions

**Appendix B:** Sample Conclusions

**Appendix C:** Two Formal Outlines

**Appendix D:** Analysis of Student Speeches in Appendix B of PUBLIC SPEAKING

**Appendix E:** Places to Find Additional Speech Texts

## Conclusion 4

". . . Although it is still sometimes difficult to sit behind the computer terminal without becoming nervous or fidgety, I am convinced it is still worth my while. I believe all of us should become comfortable with computers. Only in that way will we be able to perform in the job market and the educational system, in order to become computer literate and function effectively in our technological society."

Wanda Coppola, "Technological Society Induces Computer Anxiety," Winning Orations, p. 26.

## Conclusion 5

"Unwanted teen-age pregnancy will continue to be an unfortunate reality. But family planning clinics are at least preventing this disaster for those teen-agers who are taking responsibility for their sexuality. This new regulation could easily destroy most of what these clinics have accomplished, if we let it. The result? As one teen-age girl wrote: 'I'm seventeen and I have a three-month-old baby. If I had known that I could have attended a family planning clinic in complete confidentiality, without my parents finding out, well, I probably never would have gotten pregnant.'"

Gene Freeman, "Tattling on Teenagers," Winning Orations, p. 36.

## Conclusion 6

"Today, we've been given a brief overview of the cracks and flaws that need patching up in our public works system. We've seen how national neglect has not done as much as put a Band-Aid on the problem, and it appears that after nearly two decades of neglect, the American public has no other choice but to prepare for one expensive decade of rebuilding. Three trillion dollars over ten years is indeed a large price tag; and while at first glance the solutions I've proposed may seem dwarfed against such a high cost, their implementation is vital, nonetheless, in: one, creating the right attitude needed to tackle the problem; and two, igniting a successful thrust until additional programs and projects can be thought out and developed. Through the establishment of a national capital budget; through halting the completion of the interstate highway system; and, lastly, through state, local, and industrial endeavors to meet appropriate funding, the public works of America may soon become the thriving system it was first intended to be."

Bradley J. Ballinger, "Patching Up Our Public Works," Winning Orations, p. 42.

# APPENDIX C: TWO FORMAL OUTLINES

## SHEATHING THE SILENT KNIFE[*]

*Trevor S. Giles*

### Foundation of the Speech

Speech topic: Unnecessary cesarean sections

Specific purpose: To persuade listeners that cesarean sections have become a serious problem that requires a cure

Thematic statement: The dramatic increase in American cesarean sections over the past 20 years is the sign of a rising national epidemic, an epidemic that demands our attention.

### Superstructure of the Speech

I. Introductory Material

A. Rhetorical question: What do Julius Caesar, Shakespeare's MacDuff, and I, Trevor Giles, have in common? . . . We were all brought into this world by a cesarean section.

B. In 1963, 4.5 out of 100 babies born by cesareans.

C. In 1983, says Health magazine, 700,000 babies born by cesareans—1 out of 5 babies, a 300% increase in 20 years.

D. This dramatic increase is a sign of a rising national epidemic that demands our attention.

E. Preview: Analysis must look at:
    1. Reasons for the increase.
    2. Risks of cesareans to mother and child.
    3. Steps to return childbirth to nature.

II. Reasons for the increase

A. "Once a cesarean, always a cesarean" policy still accepted
    1. Cesarean repeat rate in America is almost 100 percent.
    2. About 80% of repeat cesarean surgeries are unnecessary (University of Cincinnati researchers).

B. Why have doctors stayed with an archaic policy?

---

[*] This speech can be found on pages 464–467 of PUBLIC SPEAKING. See also Chapter 7, Outlining Your Speech, on pages 174–197 of the text.

316

1. One reason is convenience of doctor (AMA Journal, December 1984)—an immoral and unacceptable policy.

2. Other medical reasons—fetal distress, breech babies, low birth weight, and so on—often neither accurate nor prudent (authors Cohen and Estner).

3. Most shocking reason is economic incentive.

    a. Hospitals and doctors reap $95 million per year from unnecessary cesareans.

    b. Cesareans correlate with mother's ability to pay.

    c. In 1981, Blue Cross/Blue Shield patients had 20% cesarean rate, while self-paying mothers had a 14% rate (AMA Journal).

4. Conclusion: 80% of all cesarean sections today are unnecessary (Cohen and Estner).

III. Risks of cesarean sections

  A. Why should we worry?

    1. Claim: having a cesarean is as safe and easy as getting a haircut.

    2. Answer: haircuts are not major abdominal surgery.

  B. Many potential complications from cesareans—from infection to death (Shearer)

    1. Chances of death are 26 times greater from cesarean than from natural delivery.

    2. Half of cesarean mothers experience some post-operative complications.

  C. Doctors complicate the problem by prescribing medication for pain.

    1. Two people are affected—mother and child.

    2. Mother is put in a "Catch 22" situation: either she takes medication and is too groggy to hold child, or she does not take it and is in too much pain (lay testimony).

    3. FDA does not regulate obstetrical drugs nor monitor effects on infants.

  D. Effects on child are just as dramatic.

    1. Chances of infant death are 3 to 7 times greater by cesarean delivery.

    2. Complications like wet lung, increased prematurity, and respiratory difficulties occur.

    3. Resulting separation of mother and child in first hours of infant's life impedes natural bonding process.

IV. Returning childbirth to nature

  A. Some solutions must come from medical community.

    1. Doctors must monitor their patients more closely and urge cesarean mothers to try vaginal birth next time.

    2. AMA Journal suggests that hospitals institute peer review systems for high cesarean delivery rates.

    3. Medical insurance companies must pressure medical community to bring the increase down.

B. FDA must regulate both operative and post-operative drugs for mother and child.

C. Parents must seek better education.
   1. Prospective parents must never assume the doctor knows everything.
   2. They should question their doctor about his or her cesarean rate.
   3. Parents should never assume once a cesarean, always a cesarean.

D. All these steps together can lower cesarean rate.

V. Concluding material

A. I feel the pain of my mother every time she relives the experience and the potential pain of my future wife and daughters.

B. Summary statement: The search for a solution to this problem is the search for a cure to a national epidemic that, as one author put it, has a silent knife slashing its way across the stomach of America, murdering our hopes and dreams for normal childbirth, stripping us of control, and leaving women wounded and vulnerable.

C. Concluding remarks: Let's take that knife, cure those wounds, and restore that hope, by returning the birth of children back to where it belongs: with nature.

# AS TIME GOES BY...*

*Brian Welch*

## Foundation of the Speech

Speech topic: Predicting future appearance
Specific purpose: To inform listeners how new age progression techniques allow us to predict future appearance
Thematic statement: The illustration approach and the computer enhanced technique allow us to predict how people will look as they grow older.

## Superstructure of the Speech

I. Introductory material

A. Humans have long been fascinated with an ability to foretell the future (for example, fortune cookies).

B. We now need to predict future appearances more accurately and reliably.
   1. In 1985 alone, over 700,000 children were abducted, resulting in a flood of missing children bulletins.

---

* This speech can be found on pages 467–480 of PUBLIC SPEAKING. See also Chapter 7, Outlining Your Speech, on pages 174–197 of the text.

2. These efforts are often futile because passage of time renders the bulletins inaccurate (figure one).

C. Preview: Now new age progression techniques allow us to predict how people will look as they grow older.

1. Focus on two most advanced methods--illustration approach and computer enhanced technique.

2. Look into the future of age progression.

II. Illustration approach

A. Medical illustrators Scott Barrows and Lewis Sadler first developed approach by studying facial growth patterns and using information to reconstruct an entire face from only a skull, (with clay).

B. Approach first applied to reconstructive surgery.

1. Illustrators predicted how reconstructed faces of children with congenital birth defects would look.

2. Plastic surgeons adapted more accurate procedures to reconstruct faces so that future growth wouldn't distort them.

C. Technique was then applied to search for missing children (University of Illinois Chicagoan, June 1985).

1. NBC TV asked Barrows and Sadler to create sketches for a documentary (figure two shows children used as subjects).

2. By starting with an exact tracing (figure three), 45 landmarks were identified, like eye-to-nose distance.

3. Landmarks were compared to average growth tables to sketch subject after 7 1/2 years' growth (figure four).

4. After millions of viewers see sketch on TV, girls are reunited with mother.

5. Illustrators estimate drawing (figure five) was 75% accurate, and are now conducting blind studies to hit 90–95% accuracy.

III. Computer enhanced technique

A. Conceptual artist Nancy Burson developed second technique to predict future appearance (Barry Serafin, ABC's World News Tonight, July 22, 1985).

1. Burson inspired by H. G. Wells's The Time Machine to predict how famous people will look in future (New Age Journal, October 1985).

2. Burson and computer science collaborators developed software based on her technique.

3. Technique debuted in People magazine with Brooke Shields (figure six) and John Travolta (figure seven) looking 10 years older.

B. Process involves blend of several technologies (Omni, May 1985).

1. TV camera scans photographs of subject and family members.

2. Digitizer translates information into computer language.

3. Computer software blends the photos on basis of probability.

C. Technique has promise for missing children cases.

    1. Etan Patz case typifies three cases on which Burson has worked.

       a. Etan Patz (figure eight) has been missing since 1979.

       b. Etan's picture was blended with father's and sister's photos to create possible likeness (figure nine).

    2. Unlike sketches, photographic quality of Burson's work is high.

       a. However, photographic quality does not allow for interpretation in the viewer's mind. False leads may result.

       b. In a phone interview, Burton argues her photos are in 80% accuracy range, but she has conducted no blind studies.

IV. In future, these methods may have far-reaching applications.

  A. For illustrators Barrows and Sadler, the next step is computerizing their approach to speed up the process.

    1. Interview with Barrows indicates IBM will write program.

    2. IBM will also establish computer network with law enforcement agencies.

    3. Missing children photos will be updated annually.

    4. Software may also be made available for home use.

  B. Burson is negotiating on several fronts. (People Finders magazine).

    1. FBI wants to buy her technique as an investigative tool.

    2. Plastic surgeons and patients may be interested in a new version of her program that predicts results of surgery.

    3. People in entertainment industry have offered her secret projects.

V. Concluding material

  A. Age progression is a new concept, and the jury is still deliberating.

  B. Summary statement: The applications of this technology are not only entertaining but extremely significant in the areas of plastic surgery and, most importantly, missing children.

  C. Concluding remarks: The ability to predict future appearances has now gone through the realm of fantasy into reality. As a result, we are finding that the future may be closer than we think.

## APPENDIX D: Analysis of Student Speeches in Appendix B of PUBLIC SPEAKING

### "THE RIGHT FUEL" BY THRESSIA TAYLOR (TEXT PP. 456–457)

Ms. Taylor's speech showed mastery of the analogy design. The specific purpose, thematic statement, and main points were clear. The design was easy to follow, and the analogy based upon the association between our bodies and automobiles held the audience's interest. As a nursing student, Ms. Taylor had established her speaker ethos on health issues in earlier speeches. Since the speech contained no controversial claims, it was not mandatory for her to provide support from outside sources. Had she not already established personal credibility, or had she made controversial claims, outside documentation would have been necessary.

### "ARE THE SKIES THAT FRIENDLY?" BY JULI PARDELL (TEXT PP. 458–460)

Ms. Pardell's speech was well adapted to her student audience. Her specific purpose, thematic statement, and main points were direct and clear. Her introduction included interest-arousing material and a preview of the points she would cover. Ms. Pardell documented the sources of information used in her speech. Her use of transitions was good, and her conclusion referred back to her introduction, thus providing a sense of closure.

### "THE GIFT OF LIFE" BY PAUL B. FOWLER (TEXT PP. 460–463)

By opening with two narratives, Mr. Fowler aroused the interest of the audience. These two tales of success set the stage for the contrast that was to follow and made his arguments stand out vividly. His blending of narratives, examples, information, statistics, and testimony lent strength and substance to his message. The examples and narratives helped to translate the problem into human terms for the audience. The organization of the speech flowed clearly from problem to solution. Mr. Fowler concluded the speech effectively with another narrative followed by a call to action.

### "SHEATHING THE SILENT KNIFE" BY TREVOR S. GILES (TEXT PP. 464–467)

Mr. Giles used a combination trivia-and-rhetorical question to develop an effective attention-arousing introduction for his persuasive speech against unnecessary cesarean deliveries. Since the speech was somewhat longer than most classroom efforts, he wisely included a preview of the topics. He used well-selected sources for his proof, relying on such periodicals as The Journal of the American Medical Association. His problem-solution design was clearly structured and flowed nicely from point to point. In his conclusion, Mr. Giles again stressed the importance of the problem and the necessity for action.

## "AS TIME GOES BY..." BY BRIAN WELCH (TEXT PP. 467–480)

The topic of Mr. Welch's speech was an excellent example of a subject that demanded visual aids. His audience needed to see how the age progression techniques worked. Mr. Welch opened his speech by establishing a connection between the audience's desire to see into the future and his topic; then he applied the topic to the serious problem of missing children. He clearly explained the two major methods of age progression, documenting his information with credible sources, and showed the audience just how the techniques worked, with before and after pictures. His references to his phone interview with one of the originators of the process increased his credibility. Mr. Welch skillfully related the conclusion to the introduction of the speech and brought home the practical importance of his message.

# APPENDIX E: PLACES TO FIND ADDITIONAL SPEECH TEXTS

**Regular Publications**

*Weekly Compilations of Presidential Documents* (in Government Documents section of library)
*Prize Winning Orations* (annual book)
*Representative American Speeches* (annual book)
*Vital Speeches of the Day* (weekly periodical)

**Anthologies**

Several anthologies are available in most libraries. You may wish to avoid early American and British eloquence, as the style of speaking was quite different from contemporary speech. A typical compilation, like the ones you may find in the card catalogue or COMCAT, is: O'Neill, Daniel J., comp. *Speeches by Black Americans*. Encino, Ca.: Dickenson Publishers Co., 1971.

**Indexes**

Indexes are also useful in locating speeches. Your library reference room may have sources such as: Manning, Beverly. *Index to American Women Speakers: 1828-1978*. Scarecrow Press, 1980.

**Typical Headings for Collections**

Other speech collections may be found under the headings: Speeches, Collections; After-Dinner Speeches; Forensics Orations; Oratory; or Toasts.